The Lord is my Shepherd

..iary account of West Bromwich Albion's
return to the top flight 2002 - 2003

Stefan Langford and Gavin Shepherd

First published in 2003 by
Stefan Langford & Gavin Shepherd
8 Harvington Road
Oldbury
West Midlands B68 0JF
Email: albionbook@hotmail.com

ISBN 0-9545874-0-5

Printed by Juma, 44 Wellington Street, Sheffield S1 4HD
Tel. 0114 272 0915 Fax: 0114 278 6550 Email: juma@btconnect.com

The authors wish to thank the following people for helping them compile their thoughts and experiences over the last twelve months:

Aunty Pauline / Mom
Fay
Kate
Andy Smith
Paul Smith
H
Dave
Malc
Rich
Uncle Graham / Dad
Natalie Gotting

About the authors:

Stefan Langford
Stefan is a secondary school teacher in Halesowen who has supported the Albion all his life. He lives in Quinton and has done but for 3 years at Leicester University for the past 30 years (life). Gav is his cousin.

Gavin Shepherd
Gavin is an electrician who lives in Halesowen and has also supported the Albion all his life. Cardiff University prevented him from following the Baggies for a brief spell but blue and white has been in his blood for all of his 27 years.

Prologue

Walking up to the ground was a magical experience in itself. We had already seen car after car with flags flying from windows and scarves trailing in the wind. Singing had started and we hadn't even reached Halfords Lane. Inside the ground the atmosphere was building. Quarter of an hour before kick off and chants were echoing around the arena from stand to stand. The sight was almost overwhelming. The butterflies in my stomach were only slightly depressed by an early Brandy (purely medicinal) and the weight of expectation was now beginning to tell.

The noise at kick off was deafening. Everybody shouted something. Whether it was "please God" or "come on Albion" they said something. The game was played at a pace controlled by Albion. To be honest I can't remember every detail, just those of significance. A couple of minutes in and an eerie sort of silence swept around the ground. Wolves had gone one up at Wednesday. To all Midlands football fans that last sentence has real significance but to the uninitiated it may come across as meaningless. As a point of clarity, Wolves are Albion's local and most despised rivals. To add more spice to the last day football feast, Wolves were one point behind Albion and could overtake us if they achieved a better result at the final whistle.

Less than twenty minutes in and Albion were winning. Darren "Big Dave" Moore scored from close range to send the capacity crowd at the Hawthorns wild. The season ticket holder next to me, whom I had exchanged approximately 3 words with over the last 3 years grabbed hold of my neck and shoulders and literally screamed uncontrollably down my ear. I just shouted "Yes" and jumped for joy whilst trying to free myself from my neighbour's bear hug.

Approximately 10 minutes into the second half and belief really started to set in. A Neil Clement free kick was spilled by the Palace keeper and the one and only "super" Bob Taylor scored the rebound. 2 - 0 to the Albion. News of a Wednesday equaliser, followed by a possible winner and eventually a Wolves equaliser didn't matter because after 90 odd minutes, the man in black blew his whistle and that was that.

The disappointment of last seasons play-offs gone, the indignity of having to watch third division football in the nineties forgotten, the travelling to obscure and unearthly grounds to watch your team get humbled, a distant memory and the 16 year wait, yes 16 years to see the famous blue and white stripes in the top division of English football was finally over. To me this is of extreme importance. To qualify the point, I need to explain a few facts. Last time Albion were in the top division Margaret Thatcher was only half way through her reign at number 10, Live Aid was still asking for donations, Kenny Dalglish was still top of his game, Michael Owen was at Infant school, a pint was no more than 60 pence, Steve Davis had only won three world snooker titles and Manchester United, yes good old Man U had not won the league for twenty years!!

The scenes after the match were pure theatre. The pitch invasion of noise, colour and shear happiness will stay with me forever. The bear-hugging fan next to me was not the only fully-grown man to be shamelessly crying with joy. Supporters everywhere hugged, sang, thanked the heavens and danced to their own emotional beat. The feeling of relief mixed with uncontrollable joy shocked me into a personal quiet. A time to kiss Fay and hug Gav followed. It didn't sink in and still hasn't but that afternoon was one of the happiest of my life.

Only the true football fan will understand my last thought. I say this because football is an amazing phenomenon. It's in your blood as many have said in the past. Your Dad takes you to your first match, your first kit is a birthday or Christmas present, the heroes you had at school are still in your thoughts today. Frank Skinner wrote in his autobiography that he is Albion till he dies, the only way I can describe it, is exactly the same. Just as Liverpool fans felt at winning 5 trophies last season, so Coventry fans felt at winning at Spurs to stay up some years ago. The joy Man Utd supporters felt at the Nou Camp in 1999 is the same as Kidderminster fans when securing promotion to the football league. Football is a powerful force. If you have felt it you'll know. My beloved Albion were back amongst the elite. What a day, what a future.

May 2002

It seemed as though the last headache of the last hangover had not yet cleared when the Albion forgot just exactly what they had achieved. The final game of the season was just over 2 weeks ago and the victory parade even closer in my memory but the Albion still managed to give their supporters a real life nightmare. Within a fortnight of promotion to the promised land my club had seen its chairman resign, a boardroom dispute of playground stature, rumours of Megson (the manager) leaving for another club, an EGM, and regular disagreements between supporters as to who is to blame for the farcical mess it finds itself in.

In true Albion style the club kicks you where it hurts just as you think everything is rosy. Instead of planning for the fast approaching Premiership season we found ourselves the local laughing stock once again. Paul Thomson has said he is leaving, as he cannot get on with Gary Megson, Clive Stapleton and fellow board member Barry Hurst supports his view. Jeremy Peace is the new kid on the block as it were and wants to take over from Paul Thomson and neither party seems to be prepared to listen to the other.

The bottom line is however, with less than 8 weeks to the greatest adventure and challenge in my lifetime the Albion are in-fighting, squabbling and close to turmoil.

June - July

Jeremy Peace is the new chairman of West Bromwich Albion. Clive Stapleton has resigned, Paul Thompson is still around somewhere (I think!) and now former playing star and club stalwart John Wile has left his post as chief executive. It is true to say that even for Albion this is a pretty impressive upheaval.

Brendon Batson, the assistant executive of the PFA and former Baggies full back of "3 Degrees" fame has taken Wile's place. I am not sure but I get the impression that once again we have a "different name - same person" scenario with the Albion. I say this because in recent weeks whilst second city neighbours Birmingham have spent around 7 million pounds on a proven Premiership player and the captain of a World Cup quarter finalist nation, we have secured the services of a Premiership reserve player on a Bosman free transfer! We have tried 3 times now to sign a player from Preston in the first division who was valued at over 2 million at the outset. So what does the Albion do? Initially offer 1 million plus further payments depending on appearances, then 1.5 million and finally a deal worth to be around 2 million or so the Albion say. What's the result? Preston say "fat chance" and we shrug our shoulders.

The past couple of weeks have been what I like to call "ticket office nightmare" fortnight. All Albion fans know exactly what I mean when I say this. As you can imagine, the urge for season tickets has been inevitably strong. To be fair to the club the system set up to renew your season ticket was pretty efficient. Fill in the reply slip and send a cheque, bank details etc. and leave the rest to us. After a few weeks of "leaving things to us" I got a 'phone call from my Aunt saying she has received her season ticket book with the 19 printed tickets on the right row but completely different seat number. I decided to ring the ticket office to check this as the seat she was allocated was in the "away fans only" section of the ground!!

The girl in the ticket office then had to explain to me that it had been decided by the club to switch the away section of the Smethwick End of the ground with the home section for health and safety reasons. Had it not occurred to the club to actually let the fans know? I am not sure exactly how many season ticket holders there are in the Smethwick End but I would guess at a couple of thousand. Are all of these supporters to find out they have been moved into a completely different area by word of mouth or by ringing the club in a panic? Just another piece of disastrous PR evidence to filter out of the Hawthorns. This brings me onto another side of my beloved club.

A girl at work is getting married in the summer and booked the suite at the Albion for her reception. She is a season ticket holder and was absolutely over the moon at the prospect of simply being in a place that means so much to her on a night that she will never forget. When the fixtures came out she soon realised that on the day of the reception the Albion would be at home to Leeds Utd. This would mean a little rush after the game but nothing to really worry about. Then, 5 weeks before the day Sky TV decided to make the game a pay per view spectacle. This means for some unknown and ridiculous reason we have to kick off at 5.30pm on the Saturday evening. The girl at work gets a call from the Albion saying the room she wants is now to be used for corporate entertainment after the game - read the small print regarding match time changes! No room, no reception, no compromise - no real interest to be honest. Oh, sorry my mistake, the club did offer an alternative. Smethwick ex-serviceman's club is available that night and Mild is only £1.20 a pint. How the person on the other end of the phone didn't burst out laughing when relaying the substitute venue God only knows! Our club, putting the fans first, all of the time, everytime.

Anyway, it is 4 weeks from the start of the season and I have got my passport to a year's excitement, joy and misery. My season ticket is in my draw, albeit in a completely different seat!

July - August

We have been pretty busy in the transfer market recently. Sean Gregan has finally signed for the club from Preston (perhaps it was the extra box of crisps we offered) and the Leicester City defensive-midfield forward utility player Lee Marshall (no, not the barbarian looking forward who played for Oldham in about 1970!) has also joined us. However, neither of these players were at the club for the tour of the West Country in pre-season - an opportunity to try my new tent out I told the missus who reluctantly agreed to come, eventually.

We missed the game at Exeter but travelled down to a small village called Tiverton in Devon after I had found a campsite off the Internet for our game with the small town's home team from the Dr Martins league. We found the "local" site some 9 miles outside Tiverton. It was £4.20 a night so I was chuffed even if Fay's expression as we drove past the cow shed and pigpens was less than enthusiastic.

The game saw a record crowd of well over a thousand fans

and 2 goals. There was a very relaxed atmosphere and it was nice to see the players interacting with the supporters, signing autographs and generally having a laugh. We stood in front of a group of fans from the Dudley area however, who insisted on putting on their best (or worst) Black Country accent and saying the place "Quarry bonk" over and over and loud enough to desperately get one of the locals to question them so that they could explain. Luckily no one took them up on their offer and they moved for the second half. Albion won 2 - 0 for the record, Mciness and Taylor the scorers. We found out the next day that the team coach had failed to start after the game (not like Albion is it?) so the players had to get their own taxis back to the base hotel!! It made me think, "I wonder if that would have happened to Man Utd and, if so, what would they have done? Helicopters? Private planes? Taxis?" Tiverton is a nice little place but I wouldn't recommend it to anyone who wants something to do for more than an hour or so. With this in mind I was pretty happy to pack up and head down to the English Riviera for our next match against Torquay United.

We found a campsite in Paignton a few miles out of Torquay that was a little different to our farmyard experience, shall we say. £18.50 per night was not really what I had in mind but the toilets did flush here and the other occupiers of the site were human so I booked in for 2 nights. We put the tent up and bent 14 of the 16 pegs in the process - no rain you see!! The sun shone for the 2 days, which was a record, I think, I'll have to check with the Met. Office. After spending a few hours shopping on the Saturday (sorry lads) we headed for Plainmoor. The game itself wasn't much to shout about but Albion's support was amazing really. We filled the end behind the goal and had more dotted around the place, out numbering Torquay about 3 to 1. I thought it was nice of them to charge us £10 for such an important match and the leaflet, sorry programme we shared with Charlton was definitely worth a pound of anyone's money! Albion won 1 - 0 anyway and Roberts scored. After spending the night in Paignton we headed off to Brean the next day to be closer to the final match of the tour - Bristol Rovers.

All summer I had been thinking to myself about Albion's

chances in the Premier League. "We'll be okay, we've got Gary Megson and Roberts will be fit", or "Oh my God, Chelsea's front two cost twice as much as our whole team!!" The Bristol Rovers game kind of swayed me towards the second of the two aforementioned feelings. We were two down to a poor third division side by the hour and were playing dreadfully. At 2 -2 I thought "well at least we have shown some spirit" but then Rovers scored again and I began to wonder about the opening match of the season and Van Nistlerooy and Solksjaer. I started to sweat and thought we could quite easily be down by the end of October. Perhaps this Premier league lark was not going to be as exciting after all. After boring Fay half to death with the same concerns over and over again, (we can't keep the ball, nobody in midfield can pass, there's a lack of pace in central defence, etc.) she quietly reminded me that I always said it was simply about being there as opposed to not. I composed myself, thought of playing Gillingham, Reading and Walsall and smiled contentedly - she was right. Would I have swapped Man Utd away, Leeds at home and Arsenal away for Wolves' first 3 fixtures? Not on your nelly, son. Anyway, time was ticking away and the biggest footballing adventure of my life was nearly here. Bring them on, we're "ready" (we're not), we don't fear anyone (we fear everyone). Boing-Boing!

Man Utd away

"Rob! What's that yellow light for?"....BANG!!!!That's one of the recollections from the first of hopefully many away games over the course of the next 10 months.

After a spot of car shuffling, Rob and myself, Gav, set off from Castle Road West at about 10 o'clock in the direction of Manchester. Some of Rob's colleagues at Ambi-Rad had advised us to go through Wolverhampton and avoid the chaos around Birmingham on Saturday morning on the M6.

This advice we took and after a few hours travelling we approached the M6 / M56 interchange. Several times on our journey, Rob and myself had commented on how we're only going to Old Trafford to watch the Albion and look at the ground. We're both adamant of our hate for the Man United team and supporters. Our conversation includes commenting on the distances fans travel to come to Old Trafford and how we would love to know what percentages of fans travel to the home games from different points around the country. Our views are confirmed as we overtake the South Devon MUFC Supporter's Coach.

Another familiar site when travelling to grounds is the scarf in the back window, but to take it to the extreme, one intrepid United fan had covered every window of their people carrier in MUFC stickers, scarves, flags, you name it, it was on the car! One of the delightful creatures in the back of this car had noticed my Albion top and amused himself by giving a hearty thumbs-down in our direction. Going back to our hate for the long-distance United fan, just to top it all off, we approach the junction to leave the motorway and the driver of the people carrier winds down her window and asks "Is this the exit for Old Trafford?" Typical from a United fan travelling from the south I suppose!

We continue in the traffic but take a friendly local's advice to stay off the M56 and go straight up through Altrincham. A quick change of driver as Rob's back and feet are aching and then…
"Rob! What's that yellow light for?"
"I Dunno!"

BANG!!

Clouds of steam and smoke escape from under the bonnet and there's not a lot of power from the engine. We pull over and investigate. One of the hoses has split and isn't sending the water around the engine, as it should! It's 14:40 and we both admit that we are going to miss the game!! Several bottles of water later and we seem to have cooled the engine enough to carry on our journey keeping a very careful watch on the temperature gauge.

During our roadside stay, we were approached by several footy fans who invited us to have a lift to the game and then they would drop us back to the car afterwards – these Man U fans aren't too bad I suppose!

As we approach the ground at approximately 14:55, we turn into the estate of houses nearby. Manage to park on some office frontages, due to the residents parking scheme, and start a steady jog in the direction of the ground. What's this - more friendly advice from the locals - the most direct route through the houses to the ground – "Cheers mate!"

We arrive at the ground hot, sweaty, excited, nervous, but we've missed the kick-off by 5 minutes! Nevermind, it looks very, very impressive and the Albion fans are already "raising- the-roof" (which is made of glass to let the sunlight through, thanks but I'm absolutely boiling as it is!) and creating a brilliant atmosphere.

Anyway, about the game.

Well, a really good and exciting first half – Roberts showing two defenders a clean pair of heels and then avoiding Laurent Blanc's challenge with ease. Shame about the finish though.

Albion are coping with the inevitable presence of United really well, in the midfield especially. Keane doesn't appear to be running the show, as you might expect, and I haven't heard Beckham's name once yet! Idiot, you're at the game not watching it on telly... Yes I really am watching the Albion at Old Trafford. Shame we missed the teams running out together.

Butt dances through the Albion back three and round Hoult – Oh well we knew it would happen at some point! Ha! Ha! He's hit the side netting!

Keane had a shot and a six-yard header… Van Nistlerooy and Giggs should both have converted several chances too! Good saves by Hoult and 0 – 0 at half time. Not too bad really!

Into the second half and the referee's mind must have been else-where when Balis managed to give Giggs more than a nudge in the back as he went up for a ball inside the area. For all their possession, United didn't have that edge like they had just before the break.

And then, 24 minutes to go, McInnes and Butt challenge for a loose ball with McInnes opting for the two-footed approach much to the dislike of the Man U fans and players alike. Understandable really. He DID make first contact with the ball, and I don't think there was any intent to hurt Nicky Butt, but the rules are there and it was a little over the top. Straight red! Arse!

Realistically, I think we would have gone down to ten men anyway because only minutes earlier, McInnes had been booked for time wasting on an Albion free kick which had been awarded when Keane had got a bit ratty with Sean Gregan. If not straight red, a second booking would have meant cheery-by anyway.

Wave after wave of red attacks bombarded the Albion penalty area and Moore and Hoult did everything to block shots from all angles. Enter one Ole Gunnar Solskjaer! Here we go!!! Yes the inevitable… 12 minutes from time (Off side after looking at the replays! Double Arse!) Scholes finds Solskjaer 6 yards out and Solskjaer finds the back of Hoult's net.

Substitute Super Bobby Taylor had Albion's best chance, really they're only chance of the second half, after a long ball over the top caught out Blanc and O'Shea. Unfortunately the ball bounced awkwardly in front of the veteran striker and Carroll was able to save Taylor's 12-yard effort comfortably.

Hoult made a few more vital saves to keep the score a very respectable 1 – 0 defeat. That's what happened inside the stadium. Outside the stadium is a completely different story!

We left straight after the final whistle trying to remember the route back to the car through the houses. Out the ground, turn first right, loads of Man U walking towards us. At this point I felt a push

Golden Balls in front of the Albion

in the back; I just assumed it was the crowds surging along, as you'd expect with about 30,000 all going the same way. Then someone spat on the back of my legs. Mmm, that was pleasant! I turned towards Rob who was chatting to someone. I didn't recognise him, I presumed Rob knew him. He was going on about some Munich song or something. "Where's your famous Munich song now? Eh?"
What's he on about?

Apparently, the Albion fans had been singing the Dam Busters tune with their arm out like planes; naturally, it's a song about planes! The United fans nearby had obviously thought that we were having a dig at them about Munich – who gives a shit about Munich – with all due respect. After all, it was years and years ago.
Someone else approaches, "Yeah, your not singing it out here are you? How does it go again?"

I start to go down another street on the right. This bloke follows me and I can tell he's right behind me, obviously wanting to cause trouble. He pushes me a bit as I walk down the road. Now whether I speeded up at this point, he was pissed, or he couldn't throw a punch properly doesn't really matter but he tried to hit me but only succeeded in "cuffing me" round the back of the neck. It still hurt though!

I walked round a parked van and notice three or four coppers grabbing hold of this bloke who's just hit me. He tries to get them to ask me if he hit me but I just carried on walking and let them sort it out, they must have seen something. Rob and I have now split up without realising. I turn down the first main road in the direction of the car. I start to walk with this other Albion fan who says he hasn't seen any trouble! Are you blind man!

Down past a load of coaches which I thought would be Albion fans but no, United supporters club coaches from everywhere except Manchester. More abuse. A few more Albion fans to walk with. Why did I wear my Albion top? It's a question that shouldn't need to be asked, I support my team and want to wear their shirt, but unfortunately there are some dick-heads who have to spoil it for everyone else – oh Yeah, and they don't wear their team's shirts, I wonder why? It's now ten past five; I haven't seen Rob for fifteen minutes! Where is he? Is he ok? Is he alive? A stupid question but I honestly don't know! I'll ring him…. Answer phone! I'll try again…rings for longer and then answer phone! Again… he answers but doesn't say a lot… At least he's ok.

I turn down the street I recognise from earlier, I'm sure we parked down here! United fans streaming from every street and alleyway. Time to lose the shirt, well take it of at least. I get back to the car. At least it's still in one piece; we might get home once we've fixed the earlier problem. Ring Rob again… come on… Where are you?

After much ringing, texting, panicking, praying, you name it, we met up with each other after I'd told him where I thought I was – I actually told him the wrong road name.

We start our journey back stopping at a petrol station to contact the AA via Lloyds TSB. Eventually a local mechanic bloke turned up; mind you I was asleep for most of the wait and the repairing. Not really sure what exactly was wrong, a split radiator hose or something.

Returned home not too late... I wonder if all the away games this season will have as much excitement as this before, during and after the games?!!

Leeds Utd home

Now Leeds have never really been liked by anybody outside Yorkshire have they? Their so-called great side of the 70's failed to dominate the game like the Liverpool team of the late 70's and 80's and the Man Utd sides of the 90's and the Midlands still remembers the trouble caused when they were relegated at the Hawthorns some years ago and the violence at St Andrews around the same time. Unfashionable is the term I think. So to see them roll up at the Albion with multi million pound superstars and a larger than life media's dream of a manager was a little difficult to take.

Like so many of the clubs in the English game Leeds came into the new season with money trouble. I presume it is for this reason that they sold centre half and future England captain Rio Ferdinand to fierce rivals Man Utd for a sum of around 30m pounds!! Why else would you do that? Even so they still fielded a team capable of giving Albion a good spanking. Rob had given me and Gav a lift to Junction 1 as the 3 of us had just put our tent up at Stourport for the Bank Holiday weekend. We walked to the ground along the Brummie Rd - something I had never done before and met Fay etc. in the Smethwick End as usual. The steward told us we had to walk round the East Stand to enter the Smethwick End now to avoid confrontation with away fans. As we approached our section we saw the gates that separate the home and away fans at the Smethwick end were wide open and Leeds and Albion fans freely mixed - nice one steward!

I think it's fair to say that for the first 35 minutes we gave Leeds and their millionaire stars the old fashioned run around. How we weren't at least 2 up I'll never know (I do really). During this period Johnson side footed wide from a position Helen Daniels would have scored from and Jason Roberts fired over when hitting the target seemed far easier. I repeated to myself again and again - "If we don't score when we're playing this well you know what will happen don't you?" and it did. Leeds went up the other end in their first meaningful attack and Harry "showbiz" Kewell side footed home after great work from Aussie mate Viduka. There you have it.

Albion play their best football in an attacking frame of mind, closing down like tigers in front of a near full house in the first game at home in the top flight for 16 years and go in 1 nil down at half time. That's justice for you, funny old game (up yours Greavsie).

Leeds spent much of the second half strolling around because within 5 minutes they were 2 up and the game was over. Lee "I never went to school" Bowyer scored a peach of a goal from the same area Roberts smashed over from and then Viduka sent Hoult the wrong way with a drop of the shoulder that had the whole of the Smethwick End moving to the left before he tapped in for 3 - 0. Oh dear, this is going to be a long winter I thought. This was the general consensus around too. That was what I perceived anyway until late in the game when Lee Marshall (no, not that one) scored to make it 3 -1 and the ground went wild. "We've scored - fantastic isn't it?" It was as though we had won easily outside on the way home. Fans happily chatting amongst themselves - "We've scored more than Villa and Blues put together" I heard one bloke say. Hang on a minute, we have just been well beaten by a side that didn't really try in the second half, we've played 2 got no points but we've scored a goal!! Well hot dog! Blues lost at home to Blackburn and Villa at Spurs so that softens the blow, for some anyway. Arsenal away Tuesday - piece of piss.

Arsenal away

The ground suddenly appeared out of the houses as I walked down St. Thomas' Road, then suddenly around the corner there were thousands of people making their way down Avenell Road (we think Halfords Lane gets packed!). With ticket in hand, I shuffled through the turnstile and started to walk the length of the North Bank stand (our Brummie Road end) to find my seat – right underneath the scoreboard. When I got to the top of the steps and saw the inside of the ground I was impressed, although I knew I was going to get cold, as Highbury has open corners. Apparently a new ground is being built and they're turning Highbury into flats! Best thing for it really, I hate this ground (1978, 1982 - still wiping away the semi final tears). The away fans had one third of the Clock end (our Smethwick end) and part of the West stand Lower Tier. They gave a huge cheer as the names were put up on the scoreboard (to sounds of "who?" from the home fans) and then the teams emerged onto the pitch.

Well I knew they'd get some good goals but didn't think they'd start so early – in the 3rd minute Cole scored. Arsenal were playing some classy football, showing why they were Champions last season, which shows the divide with the new teams in the Premiership. A bloke behind me commented,
"Premier and Division 1 are two different classes of football."
"Really? I never knew that mate"

Albion looked lost as Arsenal played the ball around each other and managed another two goals in the space of five minutes, Lauren in the 21st and Wiltord in the 24th. Mcinnes kept up with his tackling/fouls and received his second yellow card of the season. With about ten minutes left on the clock Albion perked up and started to play some excellent football. At one point Siggy out ran Henry to get a ball!

Half Time: Arsenal 3 West Bromwich Albion 0

Well I don't know what Megson said at half time but something clicked as Albion started the second half well. When Arsenal did manage to get near their scoring zone they were throwing their chances away with long crosses and wide shots. Albion took their chances of good play and were rewarded with a goal in the 51st minute by Dobie. The fans went wild and the singing was fantastic (I decided to join in – in my head). Couldn't get a ticket in the Albion end you see so managed to get hold of a seat with the Gooners. This gave Albion even more life and Mcinnes and Balis had opportunities to score but they were saved by the ever-present Seaman. Arsenal suddenly appeared to wake up as they started passing the ball around the whole team. It was getting a bit embarrassing for Albion as they were tackling but just couldn't make contact with the ball. All this passing around eventually paid off for Arsenal as Wiltord got his second goal in the 77th minute. But with only fifteen minutes remaining Albion got that buzz again and Roberts steered a low shot past Seaman and the post. The Albion fans were going crazy. It looked like Albion were going to leave having put up a brave fight against one of the best teams in the premiership. But just to add insult to injury, Aliadiere, who had only been on the pitch a matter of minutes, got his foot on the end of a low cross from HENRY and claimed himself an 88th minute winner.

Full Time: Arsenal 5 West Bromwich Albion 2

Didn't really think we would get anything more out of Arsenal. To be fair they gave us a hiding in parts, a proper lesson. Don't like them much to be honest with all their millionaire foreign stars and their lizard of a manager.

Fulham home

Fulham beat us at home last season in the quarter-finals of the FA Cup 1 - 0. They have been in the Premier League a few seasons now but are still beatable by all the rest really so this was a game most Albion saw as a realistic opportunity for 3 points and our first win. Prior to the game and a few hours or so before the new Premier League transfer "window" closed for 6 months, we had spent some more money on Lee Hughes' return (one time Baggies hero). Lee is a local working class lad who moved to the Albion from Kidderminster Harriers in the late 90's. He was an instant hit with his honest non-stop running for the Albion cause and the unbelievable 37 goals he scored in one season!! Albion sold him to Coventry City last season for 5million pounds and have re-signed him 12 months later for half that amount (if you believe the papers). Anyway, "Hughesy" was back to bolster the strike force and no one really complained.

Fulham being Fulham couldn't sell their 2 and half thousand allocation and had to send a thousand or so back. Now I don't know whether most fans agree with me on this point but I have little respect for a club who can't sell tickets and are poorly supported. Coming from the Midlands I feel quite strongly about this because we are constantly told how brilliant the support is in the North East etc. but you'd be hard pushed to find better support, especially away from home over a sustained period of limited success than the following of WBA, Blues and Wolves (sorry). It is for this reason that teams like Fulham can spend another 100million for me if they want but they will never be as big as us. I looked across the Smethwick End to the away section and thought "pathetic", then I saw Fulham's side with 4 British players in it at most and thought I hope we beat this "plastic" lot. Oh yeah, I wonder if Hugh Grant was at the game?

In a scrappy affair where we hustled and harried and Fulham were neat and tidy without getting anywhere we grabbed a goal through cult figure "Big Dave". We certainly deserved it and although referee Rob Styles did his best to spoil the afternoon, the boys took the points 1 - 0 and the cheers of relief around the Stadium could we be heard in Oldbury town centre. Blues had beaten Leeds earlier so we had to win in a way to save face at work on Monday morning. Jason Koumas had also come on as substitute - another last minute signing we should have completed some 6 months ago but again, more evidence that we were actually spending cash!!

Our first Premier League victory and points. We had moved off the bottom of the table and I felt genuinely hopeful and positive about what lay ahead. Teams like Everton, Southampton, Bolton, West Ham, Man City, Sunderland, Charlton and our two big city rivals can be beaten I thought. If we play with the passion and determination that Megson personifies then maybe, just maybe our obvious lack of real ability at this level can be overcome. Truth is, I was overjoyed at the result, as well as inspired, to positive thinking. The Fulham fans went home to West London and I went home to get ready for dinner at my sister and her husband's restaurant in Malvern (very posh you know, I wonder if they'll let me in? Tattoo and all). Oh yeah, sorry for shouting at you Igor, I have nothing but respect and admiration for you after what you did on Saturday.

West Ham away

"I'm forever blowing bubbles". I was blowing bubbles all right but not out of my mouth. I started the day in Bangor, North Wales and ended it in East London. To say I was knackered when I got in at 1am was an understatement of huge proportions. Gav and me drove to Upminster, as this is close to where cousin H lives. We got the tube to Upton Park, came out the station and thought we had stumbled onto the Cape - chippies, ethnic food stores, taxi HQ's, etc. everywhere. Oh yeah, thousands of people and mounted police too. One such copper announced that away fans needed to turn left here - nice, we had just walked past "here" and so had to turn round and excuse ourselves through the droves of home fans with heads down in apprehension. We got to the ground 5mins before kick off.

Night games are a little special, especially away. Hard core fans travel to places like West Ham away midweek on a night. The atmosphere was great amongst the 2800 Albion who filled the away section. The game was not the best - West Ham pretty and technically superior without really getting anywhere and the Albion strong, rugged and unsophisticated. One bright moment came however, when Jason Roberts powered past Repka and guided the ball past "England's No. 1" David James to give the Albion a one nil lead. Darren Moore was outstanding in defence and Russell Hoult as solid as a rock. There's still a concern over Clement at full back though, because when you look at it he hasn't really played well since the middle of last season!! As time ticked by I began to think about our journey back to the car. H had tipped us off about the tube, (basically if you didn't get there before the majority it could be an hours wait) so we committed the cardinal sin and left before the final whistle. I know what you're thinking but I didn't want to get in for 2am, to be up for 6.30 and sharing the tube with thousands of angry Hammers didn't attract me too much either. (It's alright if you came free on the coach isn't it?).

We jogged out the ground, past the bus depot, through the dimly lit alley (nice), down the street and onto the main street (Cape

Hill) where the station was. To our delight the queue for the tube was already out of the station, around the corner and 10 deep. We spent the next 40mins surrounded by West Ham fans who had just lost to lowly West Brom 1 - 0 at home. Neither of us spoke during this period for fear of our beautiful accents being discovered and if Gav's phone rang once it rang 10 bloody times. He turned it off. You may think this sounds a little wimpish but after the experiences of Old Trafford, Bramall Lane last season and St Andrews a few years ago we don't take any chances. We got back to the car at 10.30pm - I was knackered, Hank, relieved and feeling dirty (not like that) all at once. We drove through some of the places Tony Adams refers to in his autobiography - Hornchurch, the Chequers Pub, etc. and hit the M25 for a long journey back home.

What a night. I got in and collapsed into bed. We had our second win in a row 1 - 0 giving us 6 points from a possible 15. Survival became a little more acceptable to contemplate even though it was only 6 points, just 6 - that's 2 wins Danny "listen to me I know everything (nothing) about football because I support that massive club Millwall and I'm a gobshite from the South" Baker. Oh yeah, a nice shade of pink or crimson would suit you Rodney, you idiot.

Southampton home

This was potentially the most boring match of the season, in my opinion, but I'll try and keep you interested while you read all about it.

As we approached the ground along Halfords Lane, we notice more stewards around the entrance to the Smethwick End. Surely they weren't expecting trouble it's only Southampton after all! No, no, the Albion have changed their minds again about "the fans approach to the turnstiles".

As we are now sitting on the other side of the Smethwick End, at the first home game we thought that the gate would be shut between the home turnstiles and the away turnstiles – we were playing Leeds remember! But No… freedom to mingle! Same again for the Fulham game, and then the mighty Saints…."I think we better shut the gates for this one, John!"

So back down Halfords and along Albion Road, with many others, to join the massed ranks approaching the Smethwick via the East Stand Car Park.

Now that's me off my soapbox for a while, let's get on with the game. An encouraging start by both sides before it slowly turn into a re-enactment of what's best described as an end of season, Division 3 mid-table, nil-nil-written-all-over-it type match with the odd chance, and I mean the odd chance falling to both sides. Balis did his usual trick of working some magic down the right, getting into the box, only to completely arse up his shot/pass/cross, who knows what it was. Apart from this slight scare the visiting 'keeper didn't really have much to do in the first half. Mr. Hughes is still running round like a headless chicken and not creating much, and Mr. Roberts was either being pulled up for offside, pulled up for fouling, or being pulled over by the defender. This was all too much for the ref who finally produced a card mid-way through the half. Russell Hoult (England's Number One, England's, England's Number One) wasn't having much to do with either. Watching a shot go wide, over and relatively easily into his chest, he handled most things except at the end of the half, when, I presume a defensive mix-up enabled a lob towards the Baggies net. Fortunately Phil Gilchrist was alert enough to make a goal-line clearance to the relief of the home fans.

Half time and I think Gary Megson will either have to make some changes or give them all a right rollocking or both!

Well as the teams come out for the second half, he's definitely made two changes. Sigurdson is now in defence enabling Gregan to move back into midfield at the expense of Ronnie Wallwork. Gregan plays really well in defence, but he is more suited to midfield and their needs to be a few much challenges going in – when does Derek McInnes come back? The other change was Dobie on for Hughes. Megson made the same chance at Upton Park the other night and Scott Dobie didn't quite change the game, but he certainly made a difference!

As the second half progressed there were certainly more tackles in midfield, more chances up front but it was Southampton who had the best chance of the half. Marian Pahars managed to find his way through the Gilchrist-Moore-Sigurdson formation, which once again had shown strength when needed, only to place his feeble shot just to the left of Russell Hoult. Thank you very much, another comfortable save for Albion's Number One.

Jason Koumas is getting a little better with each game and his twisting and turning on the edge of the Saints' box made room for Jason Roberts to have a shot from 12 yards. This shot was charged down as well as his follow-up with the ball finally coming out to Sean Gregan. He steadied himself and from 30 yards cracked a shot towards goal. Not a bad effort really – even Gordon Strachan said he didn't carry on watching the ball and prepared for his next substitution. Fortunately, Paul Jones in the Southampton goal hadn't quite read the flight of the ball and managed to fumble the ball over his head and into the back of the net.

I think the fact that the ball bounced nicely, just in front of the keeper, might have confused him but we'll take all the help we can get! That could well be the goal that decides this game and to make matters worse for Southampton, Paul Williams got his second yellow card of the game after tangling with Jason Roberts again.

That’ll be red then! You are the weakest link, good bye!

A final 20-yarder kept Hoult on his toes right until the final whistle. Well, another “1-0 to the Albion”… only 15 more to go to beat last season's record and then Europe and all that Champion’s League malarkey.

“Oi, wake up ‘n smell the coffee! It’s Anfield next week!”

We can still dream though! San Siro….. Tuesday nights… small boy’s in the park… jumpers for goalposts!

Liverpool away

Liverpool Football Club, the most successful British club side of all time, an institution respected around the world - this is what being in the Premiership was all about. For Albion fans of my age this league fixture is a distant memory. For those younger than me it is to do with history books and black and white photos only, so to be travelling to Anfield was simply a dream come true.

Gav, the Smudgers, Smithy and me (no it's not an East End gangster quintet) headed for Merseyside at 10.30am on the Saturday. The M6 was moving but we had to keep stopping and starting due to the volume of traffic. It was about Stoke, at junction 16 when I first realised that the majority of cars we were passing had red football tops in them. Now I knew Man Utd were at home which would account for most fans, you would think, but the bulk of the supporters were Liverpool. As we took the M62 towards the city we saw loads more fans heading for their "home" game and even a fair number of coaches. I began to think, "I thought it was Man Utd who had the fans from Cornwall and Northampton, etc." We parked on Anfield Comp for a fiver - what a beautiful centre for education excellence that looks from the outside! Walking up to the pub by the away section of Anfield, we mixed with the Liverpool fans but one thing stuck out a mile - the lack of the Scouse accent. This was true for those we met in the pub before the game also.

The stadium was beautiful and immediately impressive. As I looked round I began to soak up the atmosphere with the following Albion contingent. Always singing, cheering and jeering, the Albion fans were a mass of blue, white, yellow and green in the bright afternoon sunshine - a sight that always excites. Liverpool fans were slowly filling the ground but there was no noise from them yet. I looked at the famous Kop opposite but because of my low, almost pitch level (row 5) viewpoint, it didn't seem anymore impressive than most ends I'd seen. 5 mins before kick-off and still no noise from Liverpool, then as the teams came out the P.A. system played the old faithful "You'll never walk alone" and a mumbling of voices accompanied it.

Anfield's famous gates - have you seen Astle's?

The game itself was dominated by Liverpool from start to end. I don't mind admitting that and the best team won 2 - 0 as well, but what got me was the poor refereeing by the one and only Mr Ellery. He gave Liverpool a penalty and sent our keeper Hoult off. No problem with that, he did rugby tackle Owen to the floor after Moore inexplicably ducked instead of heading away. But what completely stuck right up my nose was the way he bottled the penalty incident we had a few moments after the "European footballer of the year" had fluffed his. Jason Roberts added Hypia to his list of so-called top class defenders to make a fool of when the Fin decided to lunge at him from behind, miss the ball completely and swipe Roberts' legs from under him. This was seconds after tugging his shirt as he flew past him. What does the Headteacher do? Wave play on and indicate that Hypia had played the ball. What a joke. But as Megson rightly pointed out on Match of the Day - the last time a penalty was given to the opposition in front of the Kop the country was about to go to war with Mr Hitler. And ask for Hypia's arrogant response, which virtually questioned the interviewer for even daring to ask for an opinion - that stank too.

Oh well, Riser scored in injury time to make it 2 - 0 which was probably about right but I still couldn't help thinking how the game might have panned out, had we been given the penalty and scored it to go one in front. The Albion faithful were exceptional throughout but someone dropped a pin on the Kop, thankfully a bloke heard it drop and found it soon after so all was fine. We went back to the Wernley after wishing the Bristol Reds coach a safe journey home.

Blackburn home

"Good Evening Ladies and Gentlemen. Welcome to the Hawthorn's for another exciting edition of 'Premiership Referee's Big Mistakes'. Tonight it's the turn of Mark Halsey."

This should have been the announcement before the start of the game because as you read on, you'll find out why the Albion were once again on the receiving end of another refereeing blunder.
Blackburn started the game the better side with a Duff shot going sailing over the bar. Big Dave had Albion's best opening chance in the 15th minute when he powered a bullet header, inches over the bar from a Ballis free kick.

When the teams were read out prior to kick-off, there was a huge sigh of relief to hear that Yorke and Cole weren't starting the game. That was short lived as after 20 minutes Cole was introduced to replace Flitcroft.

Cole was showing his experience as he tormented the Albion defence, but they held strong, to their credit. It took a 40-yard effort, which went narrowly wide, from Tugay to get things going again and to be fair; Hoult would have been nowhere near it even if he had attempted to dive for it!

Cole created a few more chances towards the end of the half, with Thompson and Dunn providing the ammunition from midfield. This had been a very good 10 minutes-or-so for the visitors and Albion must have been relieved, as the fans were, to hear the whistle for the break.

Both teams made changes during the interval, Koumas was replaced by Marshall, and Siggy made way for Ronnie Wallwork. Guess who came on for Rovers.........? Here's a clue from the Smethwick End with chants of "Is the baby yours?" and "Jordan is a slapper!"

Now you'd have thought this would be fair enough for a few minutes to greet his arrival, but these carried on every time he got the ball. Albion started the second half much better than first and nearly had a goal from Super Bob to celebrate. Unfortunately Berg's well timed, last ditch, tackle saved the day for the Rovers.

When I said we started the second half well, I meant we REALLY started the second half well. Another chance fell to BT, which was deflected; Andy Johnson had his usual effort from about 20 yards easily saved by Freidel. Then it was Robert's turn to entertain. Twisting and turning and confusing the visiting defence he created three different chances from around the edge of the box. Freidel, again, had work to do.

But due to the lack of a rippling net, there was always the threat that these missed chances would be back to haunt us. This was almost the case half way through the half when Wallwork failed to clear properly and Yorke ended up squaring the ball across the Albion goal with no one on the end of it, what a relief.

It was Wallwork again who was involved in the action with 20 minute left, when the ref decided that Duff had been brought down and awarded a penalty. Please refer to the opening paragraph of this section again! Firstly the challenge wasn't bad enough to send Duff to the ground, and secondly if the ref was going to give a foul anyway, it was two yards outside the area! To make matters worse it was Yorke who sent Hoult the wrong way...... how he loved standing with his back towards the Albion fans pointing to his name over his shoulder – not quite sure what that was proving but still.

After Roberts kicked out at the impressive Thompson and was booked, Mego decided to send Moore up front in search of the equalizer. I think he needs to train the other defenders in the art of 'closing the gaps others leave' because with only 15 minutes remaining, Cole slotted the perfect ball to Duff who ran through the vacant hole left by Moore and found himself with only the keeper to beat. Houlty not wanting a repeat of his Anfield antics, tried in vain to reach the ball as Duff rounded him and coolly put the ball in the empty net.

A dramatic end to the match saw Dobie breeze past Berg and Johansson only to have his chip nudged out by Freidel. Johnson also had a chance during a last minute goalmouth scramble but unfortunately for the home fans nothing to shout about on this occasion – except a few expletives to the ref!

Newcastle away

220 miles, Four and a half-hours - if you're lucky. What a beautiful journey it is to the North East of England. Dave's turn to drive his People Carrier so I'm not too bothered. Now this game is on the back of a pretty humiliating defeat in the League, sorry Milk, no I mean Littlewoods, make that Rumbleows, no, Persil, Walls sausages, Netto's own face wipes, Tipton's Black Country scratchings, 10p fish bits from King's Golden Fish Bar Cup. (I'd love Albion to win it really!). The FA refused to move our game with Wigan in this competition (thanks). We requested a move because we played Blackburn on the Monday and the game with Wigan was Wednesday. "Sorry, can't help John, your not in Europe and well, your not a fashionable club are you?" Anyway, we lost 3 - 1 but Megson did rest half a dozen key players.

After a half an hour service stop and an 8-pound breakfast (that's cost not weight) we arrived in Newcastle in good time for a beer. The traffic slowed conveniently opposite the Angel of the North so I took the opportunity for a photo. I actually think it's quite impressive, smaller than I had imagined but no less impressive (sad or what?). We crossed the Tyne, which again excited me (sorry), but I was a little concerned not to see any fog, Gazza. We parked up and headed for the ground, which has got to be the closest ground to a city centre I have ever seen. Smudger put enough money in the meter to take us till Monday 8am (just in case we stayed for 2 nights!!) - nice one Andy. As I approached the ground its magnitude became instantly apparent. We walked up the steps and towards the Strawberry, as recommended by Grorty Dick. Two of the biggest bouncers on earth stood at the door of the Pub, which is always a good sign. I asked the one if it was okay for away fans to drink in here, to which he promptly replied "No". He then proceeded to point me in the direction of Newcastle Labour Club around the corner - "You'll be alreet in there lads". Fair play to him I thought. We reached the Labour Club and I went up to the bloke on the reception. "Is it okay for away fans to come in here?" I asked. He looked up from his "study of the form" and said "say that again" so I repeated

Who said we aren't cultured?

Is this close enough to the city centre?

my question in my best, deliberate Queen's English. The look on his face was as though I had said something like "Let me in, you fat bastard" by mistake. He responded by saying in the strongest Geordie accent ever "Say that again in English" - to which I had to laugh, I thought shall I talk about a black kettle and pot but decided against anymore complicated communication. I tried a final time by talking as if I was talking to a German bloke who spoke no English at all. I motioned with my hands, said the words football and Albion as often as I could and eventually he understood what I was saying, asked me to fill in the visitors slip for the Club and we went in. To say this gaff was basic is a genuine understatement but it was welcoming, served relatively cheap beer and the bloke behind the bar took down the Villa scarf to replace it with a blue and white one so it was good enough for me.

When we reached the ground after a "ham and peas puddin" sandwich (don't ask), we began the 17 flight climb to the away section. We reached the Albion level and headed for the bar. The view was impressive from this height, I swear I could see Norway. Our seats, which were on row Y (there isn't a Z), were so far from the pitch, I genuinely felt funny for about 10mins looking down. Albion filled the 3000 allocation (I'd like to see how many other teams actually do that this year) and began the usual singing. 25mins in and we go and score - wait a minute; this isn't in the script. Ballis got it, well I think that speck in the distance was Ballis. We held our own comfortably when on 45mins a cross from Bellamy I think, eluded everyone apart from Ballis. The Slovakian right back went to play the ball, which hit his foot from about 6 yards out and shot towards our goal. Murphy, who was deputising for Hoult (suspended) instinctively picked the ball up. 50,000 Geordies (no long distance fans here, mate) screamed back pass, Oh yeah, so did Alan Shearer - the Ref. had no choice really did he? I mean he couldn't use any common sense could he? If Ballis meant that as an intended back pass he is in the same defensive league as Beckenbaur and Baresi. Indirect free kick, 6 yards out, everyone on the goal line - Shearer's right boot, whack, 1 -1. Two seconds later half time. The abuse Gav and me aimed at the Ref. can't be written here because our Moms will probably be reading this eventually. I'm not sure, but I don't think he heard us as he walked off.

The second half was nip and tuck (crap) and then that man mountain of a player Solano (5ft 8) out jumped 2 Albion defenders to head the ball back to Shearer who swept it in from close range. 2-1 game over, three league defeats in a row - Blues at home next. The journey home could have been better and probably would have been but for Mr Hay. The car stank like a rabbit's hutch as Smithy broke wind intermittently and I was left to reflect on another day of motorway "food" and injustice.

See, I told you I could see Norway!

Blues home

“There’s a tavern in the town, in the town. Steve Bruce is a clown, is a clown and Karen Brady…”

Yes we all know what Karen Brady is. She’s the wife of Paul Pesci-wots-his-name! Which reminds me, I’ve just got the Albion DVD of last season. Battle of Brammall Lane and all that…… shocking!

Anyway Blues, yes, both teams started well but even though this was our first derby game of the Premiership, the build-up wasn’t as exciting as it could have been. We’ve been used to this fixture over the past few years.

Apart from a good Blues move, which saw Morrison blaze a shot high and wide from 18 yards, it was really all Albion for the first 20 minutes. Roberts hassled Tebily and Powell and after a session of corners, Albion created their best move after 10 or 12 minutes. Wallwork found Roberts who found Johnson on the edge of the area…… ALL TOGETHER NOW…….. who failed to hit the target! This is becoming quite a regular feature of the game. I’m sure someone will put a compilation together, something like “Andy Johnson’s 101 Greatest Shots Which Go Just Wide Or Just Over”.

Clement had a 30-yard free kick sail past Nico Vaesen’s post as the game progressed it got a bit scrappy, as derby games sometimes do.

On 25 minutes we were all on our feet applauding another point blank save from Hoult (come on Sven, give him a chance!) which prevented a Stern John header finding the back of the net. Straight away Roberts should have scored with a shot from the edge of the box after AJ had bravely set up the chance. Then another shot from Morrison, which as before was way off target.

Balis could have made it two in two when he charged into the area but put his shot wide of the post – it was on his “wrong” foot though! This was Albion’s last chance of the half as the whistle blew shortly after Stern John had another header just off target.

In the first half Roberts was relatively quiet but soon made up for it after 25 seconds in the second half. A 20-yard effort after a run from the halfway line tested the keeper. Megson's half-time talk must have hit home as Moore produced another fine save from the Birmingham keeper. Roberts, again, with a curler from 18 yards, and then another wide 30-yarder from Mr Johnson.

Albion's best chance of the afternoon came after about an hour when Roberts' through ball was collected wide on the left by Clement who whipped in a low cross which Marshall did well to divert towards goal. Only the quick reactions of the approaching Vaesen and his left foot stopped the Baggies celebrating the first goal.

Another good chance wasted by Hughes who beat the off-side trap but fired his shot wide of the far post. After Hughes had made way for Dobie, the "Scotsman" should have scored with his first and second touches. Roberts played him in but Vaesen saved his first shot and saw the second hit the side netting.

After another Clement free kick was saved by the visiting keeper, Hoult was called into the action as a Lazaridis cross caused havoc in the goalmouth, with Horsefield hitting the post, a Morrison shot cleared off the line and John heading straight at Russell Hoult. But this was just the beginning of the end, if you see what I mean.

With only ten minutes left, Tebily got his marching orders after a wrestling match with Roberts on the edge of the area. I'm not sure if it was straight red, but he had been booked in the first half so he had to go anyway!

Then AJ's aim got a little better when his shot, after a scramble in the visitors' box, was cleared off the line. Then almost immediately at the other end, a cross from Powell deflected off Gregan, hit the near post, bounced off Hoult's shoulder, cannoned off Big Dave's shin and into the back of the net! What a bummer!! Nevermind, we continued to press on and it paid off. With only minutes remaining on the clock, Roberts received the ball on the left of the area, evaded the challenge from Vickers and curled a beauty into the far corner.

Rapid!

It was as though we had won!!

Chelsea away

After a few pre-match drinks in the Black Bird, we made our way to Chelsea Village. It's down here somewhere. Yes, here it is with the most elaborate fish & chip shop you've ever seen.

Baddiel and Skinner were on view but all the Albion fans were swarming around Frank. I think the Chelsea fans must get used to seeing the celebs in that part of the country. Photos all round... how small is Frank!

A good start from the Baggies and an early counter attack saw a Dobie attempt prevented by World Cup Winner Desailly. Roberts then had a relatively feeble shot saved by Cudicini. He really needs to improve those left foot shots!

Chelsea's team was full of experienced internationals and this extra class was obvious as they showed the Albion how a team should pass and keep the ball. Then a pinpoint through ball from Petit enabled Zola to set up Hasselbaink with a great opportunity to beat Hoult, but once again the Albion keeper came out on top and forced the Dutchman wide.

Another clever ball from Petit allowed Hasselbaink to elude the Baggies offside trap and he raced forward to beat Hoult even though his shot went in off the keeper's leg. Petit, who was in total control of the midfield, would probably have done just as well without the assistance of Frank Lampard. Marshall, Johnson and McInnes seemed to be running round in circles for most of the half. A last gasp tackle stopped Petit extending the lead and Zola should also have done better soon after. Once again, Roberts only managed a handful of half chances but unfortunately these were Albion's best of the first half!

As the second half started it wasn't long before Chelsea were carrying on from where they left off. Gronkjaer did well to beat Moore, but the defender did better still to recover and block the shot. Wave after wave of pressure and it took only eight or nine minutes for the alarm bells to ring for the second time. Jimmy Floyd Hasselbaink seemed to waltz into the area and danced around Balis and Moore. Gilchrist blocked his shot on the line, but unfortunately Graeme Le Socks was unmarked on the penalty spot and gladly made the most of the opportunity.

Megson rallied the troops by introducing Hughes after an hour, replacing the tired-looking, ineffective Marshall. He should have done this earlier. AJ must have changed his attacking tactics to headering. He timed his run to perfection and met Clement's corner perfectly. Fortunately for Chelsea the upright was to their advantage even though the keeper was rooted to the spot. Seconds later, as Albion broke down a Chelsea counter attack, Clement's 35 yard thunder bolt struck the bar and fell nicely into Cudicini's arms.

Even though it seemed like Chelsea had taken their foot off the pedal a little, they showed they were more than capable of creating a chance when required. Zola should have made it three but sent his shot high over the Albion bar. Hughes then broke free again but the keeper was equal to his shot at the near post.

Albion had their chances to get back into the game but Chelsea never seemed to look troubled and always had something else up their sleeve. We trudged back to the tube station after yet another poor display. Took one last look at the £2.80-a-pint pub and headed for the car on the Picadilly line. London, who would live there out of choice? Time to start panicking I feel. We played division one football today, no mistake about that. Chelsea are a very good side but we would have struggled to beat their pensioners today! Just thought I'd give Shaft a mention at this point. He is a black dude who I used to play football with on a Sunday. He is a big Chelsea fan from Smethwick!! He was our prolific number 9 who had a similar goal ratio to Robert Rosario (3 in 4 years) but to see him in the Albion end made me laugh after all these years. He used to say he had a ticket for Chelsea's games but had to give it away or sell it because of other commitments. Yeah right Shaft.

Man City home

Now having lost our last 5 games or so, not counting the point against the Blues, this game became rather important shall we say. Man City are not the best team in the division by any stretch of the imagination so if we are truly going to stay up, this is a game we really should win. Looking at the fixture I would normally be quite positive but after witnessing the awful Chelsea performance, to add to the inept shows against the Blues and Blackburn, I was not really too confident.

Gav was doing some electrical something or other so didn't go and Vince had his "gold dust" ticket! We went down the Wernley for a couple before the game then headed off. The news in the car on the way to the game didn't exactly fill me with hope. Now I've never questioned Megson's selections because, well, what he did last year elevates him to God like (Cyrille Regis) status but I simply could not understand a midfield of McInnes, Johnson and Chambers. McInnes is slow, can't pass but is a trier (and club captain), Johnson is a workaholic, a superman but also lacks a little craft and Chambers, who hasn't started a game all year incidentally, is energetic but again, low on creativity and skill. How on earth was a midfield such as that ever going to create chances for Roberts and Mr A. N. Other? Answer: it didn't!!

Half way through the game and I'm thinking, "first to score will win this". In other words, this is crap and one goal will be enough for either side. Man City are weak defensively (a Kevin Keegan side poor at the back? Never). Perhaps they should recruit Mark Lawrenson as their defensive technical coach. Remember that? What a joke Newcastle. Spent at the back they might be, but going forward City were far superior and clinical. Pass and move (that's weird isn't it?) and Albion's defence was all at sea. 1 - 0, Anelka. Apparently he's worth 30 million now, well that's what his brother said. We rallied for a bit, then the headteacher gave us a free kick for the 4000th foul on Jason Roberts. That annoying little dick Berkovic refused to go back 10yards so was promptly booked and the headteacher moved us 10yards closer to the City goal. Up steps

Clement, who last played well when the Royal Engineers won the FA Cup after playing 2 games to get to the final (just joking Neil, I think) and hammers it home for 1 - 1. Real chance now we can use this momentum and go on to win the game. Yeah right. After an almost carbon copy of the first City goal (that's a reference to photocopying, not the former Albion defender who was once famously quoted as saying, "if we go down, I'm off". Yes, if we go down Carbon, too bloody right you're off) they go and score a second through Goater. City go wild, we huff and puff and fail to blow any house down. Lost 2 -1. No creativity, no invention and no Jason Koumas in Midfield. Why, Megson?

City celebrate like they have won the league, sing a song about United (why they honestly do this I'll never know because it's the equivalent of Halesowen Town chanting about the Albion). We trudge off, 2 points off the bottom of the table, having to go to Bolton who occupy this place next week. I now honestly believe we may not be good enough. Played 12, lost 8, scored 9 are the worrying stats but what they don't tell you, is the way we are playing. Heart, passion and endeavour will only get you so far. It maybe just short of 17th in the Premier League.

Bolton away

This is a game we just had to win. Not really, I suppose but we could really do with one. Dave picked us up at around 10 Saturday morning and we headed off for the M6. After a BK breakfast, (the real food was over the bridge which was just too much to handle for a Saturday morning) we got to the mass of metal stanchions with no character at all (that's the Reebok Stadium, to most of you) by 12 midday. Before I go any further I must just give a mention to the bloke on the services who called me over to his car and said, in the best broken Italian/English accent I have heard since Alexis Sayle did Mussolini in the Young Ones, "Hello, me and my partner (who said nothing and looked like a character from Goodfellas), are importers from Eeetaly. We are specialise in fine Eeetalian leather coats (he is stroking the collar of his own very shiny PVC black coat at this point). Would you liking to see some...?" I stop him at this point and politely say that I am very happy with the coat that I have got, thanks anyway!

The shopping area by the ground is home to 2 pubs. At the first you are required to show a home ticket just to get in so not surprisingly we went to the second. After ignoring the "no away fans" sign we soon realised that this was actually a 10 pin-bowling place that had a bar and one barman and loads of Albion already. We doubled up on the first round and picked the bones out of the season so far. After 5 mins we had finished that and spoke about something else! Burge came in and said he had just tried to get in the first pub by doing his best "Bolton accent". I thought about this for a minute and realised just how impossible that task was. You know, the famous accents of the nation, Cockney, Brummie, Scouse, Geordie, "Boltonian". Needless to say, he was turned away, point blank.

We were in the lower tier next to the home fans. The game started well for the Baggies and Dobie scored on about 15mins with a screaming volley from the edge of the area. 2 minutes later the imported centre half N'gotty, I believe his name is, was the nth defender to be unable to handle Roberts and promptly elbowed him in the face. Goodbye. Bolton down to 10 men, we're 1 - 0 up, they

Super Bowl XXXII

are bottom, what a dream. For the next 65minutes we had one chance and played crap to be perfectly honest. We are quickly becoming the poorest footballing side in the division. Nobody in midfield is capable of passing the ball, defenders get rid of the hot potato ASAP and unless Roberts beats 5 men and scores, we don't!! Megson seems to instil a fear amongst the players that if they try to keep the ball, we'll get beat. We didn't attack at all in the second half when a second goal would have killed Bolton for sure. We sat back; allowed them to attack us, which they did, to their credit and on 88mins duly equalised with a Fransen header. Sick to the bottom of my stomach, I was. Bolton celebrated by singing "You're going down with the Villa" which seemed a little ironic considering a point still left them bottom and Villa were beating Fulham 3 - 1. We trudged out of the ground and back to the car. We all definitely agreed relegation is a certainty if we continue to be so negative and basic in the way we play the game. No Ref. to blame, no injustices to bleat about. Simply not good enough. Am I really questioning Gary Megson? Never thought I'd do that but the way we are playing is frightening. Survival is our goal though and if we achieve it, I'll be amazed but I won't complain about the standard of football we play if we do!

Oh yeah, just a little footnote to mention the hideous woman in the Bolton section at the end of the game. She was having a personal run-in with what seemed like all the Albion fans. Sticking the V's up, shouting F - off, motioning to fight, frothing at the mouth - totally out of control. All this whilst she tried to hold the hands of her 2 young children. They must be so proud of you, love. The Vile next - I can't bear it!

Aston Villa home

Now for me, this is the game. Forget Wolves (I never met a Wolves fan until I was 20 and before that, we just used to feel sorry for them, a bit like Walsall). Blues have always been similar to us in many ways and poor relations (honours) in others so they never really bother me either. Living where I do on the Western edge of Birmingham, close to the Black Country border you either support Albion or, if you are just inside the border (Quinton) Villa. I first started going to games in the early 80's when Wolves played on a Friday night in front of 5000, Blues were an average to poor top flight side, we had the end of what was once called the most entertaining side in England (Regis, Robson, Cunningham, etc.) and Villa were league champions. Just to put it into perspective, when Villa won the 1981 title we actually had a chance ourselves with about 5 games to go. We narrowly lost to them 1 - 0, then did them a huge favour by beating eventual runners up Ipswich 3 - 1. Basically at my junior and senior schools you either wore claret and blue or the famous blue and white stripes. I proudly wore the latter and can still remember crying having lost 1 - 0 to the Villa and having to go to school the next day to endure weeks of torture. Since then I have met about 3 true Wolves fans (they rarely venture south east to the metropolis), 10 Blues but countless Villa. So, 20 years on from the start of me really supporting the boys, the burning hatred of our big city neighbours still rages inside.

During the lean spell and dark days of the late eighties and the entire nineties Villa, with the exception of one blip remained a top division side. Whilst we were losing to Woking they were playing in front of 30,000 and against Liverpool, et al. Living where I do this meant we slowly became a joke. No more chanting about the Albion at Villa Park because well, who were they? "Poor little Albion, I would like to see them do well" was probably uttered many times amongst the Birmingham section of Villa supporters. We had missed a generation. Lost our presence. Quite simply, there was no rivalry between the clubs at all. Just memories of supporters aged 25 and over. Rivalry and hate (this is not used lightly) is built up over a long period. It is based on memories and incidents. Living your life amongst the supporters of the team you dislike most fuels the feeling. How strange it is to have some of your best mates ever, family even, supporting the others. I know loads of Villa fans, some I am very close to and have shared many great times with (Brandhall Rovers) but if asked who I hate the most I answer without any hesitation, Aston Villa. I still recall Brendon Batson's back pass, Gary Robson's broken leg, Warren Aspinall's winner, Alan Evans' stupid sweatbands, Bayern Munich's complete dominance in Rotterdam and the faces on countless school mates after having lost again. So, here we are 16 years later and West Bromwich Albion versus Aston Villa is a fixture in the top division in England again.

To say I was anxious on the Saturday morning was similar to your mom saying "Do you think there will be many up there today?" Vince and me had breakfast then headed to the Wernley with Fay. After a couple we went to the game. There must have been hundreds, no thousands of blokes like me that morning. This was the game. Panic, anxiety, fear, excitement - the lot. It meant so much. You hear little stories to prove it, like when I found out a load of mates I used to play football with actually booked a gym and had an Albion - Villa 6 a side match before the pub!! I think they are still talking and walking.

Now I know it has been a long time since we last played and to prove it many Villa fans thought they were in the old away section of the Smethwick End. We were walking down Middlemore when a small bunch of lads came out the tram station and started singing Villa songs. They were right behind me and I instantly felt the hairs on my neck extend. When we got to the entrance to the "Avenue", the stewards sent them back the other way and I found myself without any thought at all half saying, half shouting "Yeah piss off round the other side". The missus looked at me as if to say, have you gone completely mad? As I walked towards the ground, I thought bloody hell you better calm down.

There was already a great atmosphere building inside. I looked at the menu and was drawn towards the Brandy but remembered the £3.50 price tag so steadied my nerves from within. Seeing the claret and blue walk out with the famous stripes brought back so many memories. The fact that we were already staring relegation in the face was lost on me for 90mins. I spent much of the game on my feet, which is rare at Home and must take this opportunity, even though it is a cop-out, to apologise to my Aunt for my behaviour and foul language throughout the game. The match itself was a contest between two poor sides, a million miles from the battles of the early eighties. Jason Roberts should have scored twice in the first 20 mins and God only knows what I would have done if he had. Second half was mainly them and then with about 15mins to go, my heart sank to the floor. Big Dave was judged to have felled Barry in the area and the Ref. seemed to point to the spot in slow motion. That was it. All over. Try and prepare yourself for the aftermath because there is no way they're going to miss this right in front of me! Dublin steps up, small run up, doesn't look too confident. Dummies then fires low and hard straight down the middle. Hoult dives slightly to his right and saves the shot with his legs. A Villa player then hits the ball out of play. Goal kick to the Albion. Pandemonium. It is as though we had scored. The last 10 mins were awful. At the final whistle I was relieved more than anything that it was all over.

That was that. More memories to add to the bank. Pity we didn't score and more importantly win (we are now bottom as Bolton have just beaten Leeds at Elland Road - nice one El Tel). I went back to the pub to ponder on what might have been and to calm down!! Oh well, we do it all again in four weeks down at Villa Park. Swoff says he'll take us with him to some working men's club he uses over Aston before the game. That should be nice.

Incidentally, I feel it is necessary to mention at this point, a bet me, Dave and Smithy had in the middle of last season. We all agreed (In the belief that there was no chance) that if Albion got promoted we would have a tattoo. As the season drew to its close, the possibility of a tattoo became more and more real. After the Palace game it was decision time. Fay wasn't really up for it if I'm honest and I was a little reluctant. I mean, how many teachers do you know with a big football crest tattooed on their arm? We left it for a couple of weeks, then Vince said he fancied a target tattoo, so me, him and Gav went up Bearwood to have a look at "Tommo's Tattoos". I hadn't seen Dave or Smithy since the match so had no pressure on me really. I looked at the catalogue of tattoos and as sad as it sounds, loved the Albion shield. Vince had made up his mind to have a target drawn up and the outline placed on his arm. I still wasn't sure. I paced up and down the shop and thought of everything possible. Sorry lads but I have to admit that I went outside and rang the missus. I told her that Vince was in the chair having his now and she said, "Well, if you said you we're going to have one and if he is now, you can't back out!" That was that. In her reply was a definite blessing. Right? I went back inside and boldly said OK mate let's do it. I sat in the dentist's chair (seriously) and removed my top (steady girls). The expert traced the outline of the famous shield and sorted his colours out. Red, green, brown and blue of course. He started drawing the outline in a dark colour. This tingled at first then smarted until I could hardly feel my right arm. The bloke continually wiped away the blood and cracked jokes to reassure me (total waste of time). After 30mins it was done. He put the tissue on my arm and some cellotape as a sort of big plaster and took the £50 with a big grin. He said he was red hot at the Albion shield, as this was about the tenth he had done this week!! So there I was, standing on Three Shires Oak Road with a life-long symbol of my devotion to the Baggies. My right arm still felt numb but I was happy (worried sick) with what I had done. Showing Fay was okay because of the phone call (clever or what?) but now I had to show the Queen. Sunday morning I went down home and showed my dad in the garden. He was okay with it. Then I paced up and down the kitchen trying to listen to the conversation my mom was having with me (not one word). Eventually, I simply pulled my sleeve up and showed her. Her reaction was priceless. She frowned, came closer for a good inspection and said "What a crappy colour". I just couldn't believe it. Anyway Dave and Smithy still haven't kept their ends of the bet but I'm not too bothered because as daft as it sounds I am dead proud of it.

Everton away

Big weekend this is gonna be. Vince's birthday Friday night, Albion Saturday, all going out Saturday night when we get back. Glad it's pay day next week!! Gav's turn to drive to Goodison but he hasn't started his Golf for about 3 years so don't hold your breath, I thought. True to form, I get a phone call from Gav on the Friday saying his breaks are shagged so it will probably be better not to risk it, good choice, I felt. I said he could drive mine, then on the Saturday morning as I went to the bank, the exhaust began to make a noise like a vibrating tin lid so that was out too!! Nice! Luckily Fay had just had the MOT on her car passed that morning so I asked her nicely whilst she was still asleep and she muttered something like yes, so off we went.

Now everyone knows that Everton are the true team on Merseyside don't they? No long distant "foreign" fans here mate. Scousers all the way. They had won their last 5 games on the spin so it was a pretty daunting task for anyone, let alone a struggling Baggies side. We did the customary predictions in the car on the motorway. Only Gav had us down to win, I just couldn't see it, to be honest. After the usual breakfast at the services, (best part of 10 quid including a cup of tea!!) we reached Liverpool in good time for the Man Utd - Newcastle game. We drove round Goodison twice until we decided to park on the secure car park by Anfield. We had a few beers in the Archal whilst watching the match (I dropped me ham cob at the bar which caused a bit of confusion at one point but I found it again, close one that). At about quarter past 2 we headed off for the ground. Walking past Anfield, Gav took a photo of the famous gates and eternal flame whilst I froze at the thought of living in one particular terraced street. It was the most amazing sight I have ever seen. I thought the Brandhall Estate was rough but this took the biscuit. At least 10 houses were boarded up with burnt wood and the charcoal remains decorated the window frames and walls. Then on its own, a single car outside a single inhabited home. Unbelievable! A whole street had been abandoned and torched. It started me thinking about life in the inner city and the poverty that

Everton away section - worst view in football

must exist for some, ironic really, as that week I had been discussing life in the Brazilian Shanty towns with Year 8 and this was a bloody sight worse!!

The grimness continued outside the ground with the worst burger I have come into contact with since the one which resulted in a week of diarrhoea whilst at University in Leicester. I was a little suspicious of the grey/yellow colour and the rancid smell of the stall itself. After 3 bites (it did cost me 2 quid) I volleyed it into the nearest bin. We found our turnstile and made our way to our seats. Gav went in front then turned and said, "We're only on the back bloody row again!" I couldn't get me breath. The away section at Goodison is now officially the worst view in the Premier so far. "Shove them up there in the wooden seats where their view is restricted by a huge metal stansion" - this seems to be the attitude. Awful view, right in the corner too. The game was nothing to shout about but fair play to Everton, the atmosphere was much better than at Anfield. Albion were predictable and lacked ideas (heard that before somewhere). It was no surprise to see Radzinski put them one nil up after about half an hour. We rallied briefly and should have equalised when Roberts was clean through but he fluffed his lines again I am afraid to say and that was that. Albion slump to the bottom of the league and a hard working, very average Everton side go third!! Not another motorway journey to suffer I thought - crap food, foul stench in the car, 2 hours and nothing to shout about because Blues scored in the last minute to win at Sunderland, Villa thumped West Ham 4 and even the Dingles got a lucky 2 - 1 win. Would you believe it? One thing all of us in the car did believe, however, is Albion are a certainty to go down if things continue the way they are, bust-up or no bust-up Messers Hughes and Megson. Oh yeah, just a thought for the heavily made up Scouse woman who was laughing at me after the game and saying ridiculous things like "poor little Baggies" and "Bless 'em" … Piss off.

I'm just going to be a little boring now and comment upon the social change that Merseyside must have experienced over the last 20 years. I have come to the conclusion, that as a result of harsh economic conditions in the 70s and 80s people must have left Scouseland in their droves in search of work and a better life. I say this because after the game loads of Everton coaches were lined up to take the fans all over the place. At the services we met more Everton fans in Stafford than Albion! Fair play though, loyal to their team as always. I wonder if there are loads of Albion at the services when we are at home? Don't think so, because although the West Midlands suffered industrial decline, I don't think it was as hard hitting as say, Liverpool, the North East, Glasgow or Belfast. Everywhere you go you meet a Scouser or a Jock working away don't you? Must have been grim though, having to leave, I've got respect for that.

Middlesborough home

For the first time in ages, the Baggies started today's game attacking the Brummie Road End. Having said that it was Boro who could have had the first real chance right at the start. Fortunately Siggy got in the way with a well-timed header before the aging, but still lethal, Boksic could get on the end of an interception. Koumas was the main Albion threat, as he plays more at this level you can certainly see the difference he gives to the Albion side. Jinxing his way across the field, one, two, three.... He doesn't mind how many he takes on; until he's brought down on the edge of the box. Cue Clement...

Schwarzer had only minutes earlier, seen a Clement Cruise Missile hit the outside of his post, so I dread to think what was going through his mind now? Straight at the keeper's chest and not one Albion player following in. Typical.

Koumas again and then a Balis precision cross from the right which Clement had difficulty keeping under the bar. Boro, to be fair, were giving Albion a lesson in keep-ball at times, but they could keep possession all they liked 'cause they weren't getting anywhere!

Albion's attack then looked more like a circus as Roberts miss-hit Balis' cross, which fell to Johnson who slipped as he hit his shot and the ball trickled aimlessly towards the goal. Johnson soon made up for his previous effort by bringing out another excellent save from Schwarzer after a good run and 25 yard shot. No real efforts on goal from Boro. I bet Houlty couldn't believe it.

The start of the second half was extremely entertaining, for a neutral. Roberts nearly scored virtually from the kick-off, only for Ugo Agoogo Eihugogogogoo to take the ball, literally, off his head. THEN straight down the other end, Shaun Gregan, king of the Let's-try-and-score-as-many-own-goals-as-I-can competition, slices another clearance for the second week running. Now I know he's only playing in defence because Gilchrist is injured, but he's a right-footed midfielder. Why is he on the left in defence?

A chance went begging for Boro in a slight let up in Albion's domination but Ugo failed to make something of a free header at a rare Boro corner.

Then, yet another chance to Albion, Gregan with a follow-up shot to his cleared header towards goal. 12 yards out put a goal was prevented by yet another magnificent save. Are we ever going to score?

Hughes left the field to rapturous applause, not sure why, to be replaced by Dichio. Balis found Koumas who almost opened his goal scoring account with a delightfully curling left-foot shot. Just wide with the keeper left standing. Next the two wingbacks combined yet again. Balis saw his shot go just over as he connected first-time with a Clement cross.

Roberts was back to his old ways shortly after, running Southgate ragged from the half way line to the area, but Schwarzer collected his shot. Headers followed from Dichio and Sigurdsson. And it was a Dichio-Siggy combination, which created Albion's deserved goal. Moore unfortunately blocked a shot from Siggy but the rebound fell nicely to Dichio who slotted the ball into the back of the net. About time!! Only 15 minutes or so left, it would have been an injustice not to take all three points from this game. Nothing silly now, Albion!

Oh no, 8 minutes to go, Boro head the ball against the bar. Don't let them back in now, Albion. Horrifyingly, as the Boro player connected with the ball he clashed heads with Big Dave. Now you'll probably know by now, Big Dave is, well, big. Very nice bloke, honest Christian and all that, but at the end of the day, he is a BIG bloke. After a few minutes Big Dave (Darren Moore to the still wondering) was on his feet but unsteady. Joseph Desire-Job was life-less, I mean not moving at all, and then his shoulder started to twitch! Sickening I know, one minute your playing football, next minute… well it wasn't what it could have been, fortunately, and he regained consciousness in the ambulance on the way to hospital.

When we were discussing this book, we couldn't decide whether we should have an age certification on the cover. Couldn't decide how far we were allowed to go with swearing!

Mind you, after that last paragraph I think it might nearly

have been an Eighteen! It was shocking though!

Sorry, back to the game. Boro had to finish the game with 10 men because they had used all of their subs earlier in the game. Due to the lengthy pause in the game we had to endure six minutes of injury time in which Albion didn't really attack at all and Whelan nearly spoiled the day by hitting Russell Hoult's bar with seconds to spare. But the players held on, to earn three deserved points.

Hope that blokes all right!

Spurs away

Felt it necessary to write about the weekend itself before this game, as it was pretty hectic, shall we say. Friday night Tez, Gav and me decided to go to France on a booze run. After spending an hour or so on the Net (with no joy surprisingly) we just agreed to go to Dover on the off chance and see what's what. We picked Gav up just before 4am Saturday morning and headed off for Dover. Two and half hours later we had one of the worst breakfasts (there has been a few lately!) ever at some services on the M20 in Kent I think. Cold this, cold that, 6 quid, you know what I'm talking about don't you? Well, anyway, with about 2 miles to go before getting into Dover I could see the sea. I think it was this sight that triggered something in my brain (we Brummies don't see the coast often!). "Have you got your passports?" I asked. "No, have you?" was the reply. "No" I said. "You don't need 'em do you?" Now let me think about that one. Travelling abroad to a foreign country? Passport? Don't be silly! I couldn't believe it. Brummies are said to sound thick, aren't they, but the woman I spoke to at the desk at the ferry passenger lounge must have thought she'd heard it all. Don't forget, we had been up four and a half-hours, travelled 200miles at a cost of 40quid petrol, only to remember our bloody passports spitting distance from the Channel! Now for the part where you finally realise that Brummies are pretty daft. We got back in the car, took it in turns to drive back to Oldbury via Halesowen, had another fry-up, a lot better this time (cheers Trine) got our passports and wait for it, drove all the way back down to Dover again!! By the time we got back home it was 2am Sunday morning, Gav had worked out that we had travelled the equivalent distance as Cornwall to Northern Scotland (no joke - check it). We had spent a fortune (not just on petrol either) but had a proper laugh. The story about the joke fart machine and the French lady in the lift is too painful to tell but needless to say, it will be in the future over and over!

“We might as well go now!”

I’m sure this thought must have been going through the minds of most of the Albion fans before they had even got comfortable in their seats.

Well this Spurs lot are always trying to out-do their Arsenal rivals but why is it the Albion, who have to suffer an early goal again. Three minutes for the Gunners and now Spurs have done it in two!

A very dodgy free kick awarded to Teddy Sheringham on the edge of the box gave Clement the chance to show off his skills of running from the goal line to the six-yard line and back and back again and back again. Neil – just stand still and if the ball comes near you........ Oh well too late, it's in the back of the net. Christian Zeige's free kick puts Spurs one nil up.

This did however give Albion even more incentive to attack, I must admit! Jason Koumas' quick break found Hughes on the right who put in a perfect low cross, which evaded everyone including the out-stretched boot of Johnson. Ballis then found Roberts who rounded the keeper and then only managed to clear the bar from a tight angle.

After about quarter of an hour, it was Roberts' turn to play in Ballis on the right. His inch perfect cross was latched onto by Clement's left boot and he promptly broke the back of the net from five yards out..... No don't be stupid, he somehow put it wide from five yards out! That's where your right foot comes in useful; you know the one on the end of your OTHER leg!

It really was all Albion, I know that seems hard to grasp but it really was. For the first half-hour it was one attack after another and the majority of them were started by Koumas, one way or another. A little mazy run, a neat through ball, all the things we've been missing for a long time.

After a run which started deep in his own half and ended at the home side's area and which must have left at least four opponents dizzy, Koumas played the ball to Hughes but his tame shot was easily saved by Keller. Then Koumas showed he has an eye for goal, as he connected with a loose ball at the edge of the box only denied by a full stretch save by the American keeper.

Then the killer blow, the sucker punch, but really we all knew he would. Bloody Dingle reject. A neat couple of triangular passes and a quick ball over Keane's shoulder for him to run onto and beat the Baggies offside trap. I'm sure Gregan must have felt like bringing him down as he made chase but he would have definitely walked. Into the area, quick side step and a flick with the outside of the boot and Hoult is left grasping thin air. The usual cartwheel-type-backflip-type-thing, right in front of the annoyed Albion faithful, and much cupping of ears. (I've just read that this little celebration has got Mr. Keane into trouble with the FA – silly boy!) Two nil… come on Albion, you don't deserve this.

A Clement free kick flew inches wide of the target before another Koumas drive went sailing over the bar. Then Keane was sent clear again, he really has got this back line sussed. Fortunately for Albion, Hoult had come out and managed to get a body part to the ball and deflect it over the bar.

Shortly after the restart, Shaun Gregan chalked up another attempt at goal. Unfortunately, he does like to worry Hoult and the rest of the fans by slicing at least one effort each game very near to the Albion goal. Another shot from Keane, which is blocked in the more conventional manner by Gregan. Then, the incident of the game.

Hughes is subbed for Dobie and his first chance of the action is presented to him on a plate by Koumas. Another inch perfect ball beats the Spurs back line allowing Dobie to race clear. At this point the keeper realises he needs to take action and proceeds to come out of his goal, out of his area to try and clear the ball, ok that's fine, but next time try and actually make contact with the ball and not with our striker! Surely he's got to go for that! No, the ref is taking far too long to do anything, in most cases - like at the other end of the pitch – he would have produced a straight red card…. I'll have a word with the linesman… WHAT – JUST SEND HIM OFF…. Yellow, bloody yellow…. "You don't know what you're doing" and songs alike soon fill the air! The following Koumas free kick was, of course, saved by Keller who prevented the ball from reaching the bottom corner.

Then with only 15 minutes or so left, super sub Dobie managed to break free from the restraints of Richards and charge forward down the right before unleashing a missile from the corner of the box into the far of Keller's goal. Cracking! Now come on...... I'm not really sure if Hughes was right to come back to the Albion, but he definitely isn't the player that he was a few years ago. It's a good job Dobie is causing so much havoc when he comes on, I wonder if he'll get a run from the start against Villa?

Clement then wasted another opportunity to bring Albion level but he headed over from a few yards out after a Koumas corner. This was Albion's last real attack of the game, shortly before a scramble in front of Hoult's goal gave Poyet the chance to find the net with his first touch of the ball. The ball fell to him after persistence from Iverson had paid off and Wallwork and Sigurdson had failed to clear.

Oh well......... a ridiculous goal, a well-worked goal, and a scramble. Three goals, three clear-cut chances. I guess Albion have got to realise that possession and creating chances doesn't win any awards at this level, even if it does get you a few more mentions from the Sky team.

Roll on Villa...........

Aston Villa away

Away at Villa - the game of the season for me. The game of a lifetime, it could turn out to be. You see the last time we played the vile in the top division my dad said I was too young to go - I was, (I am 29 now!!). If we go down, which is pretty likely at the moment, we may never play them again so I will say it again, the game of a lifetime. Now it has already been documented earlier that AVFC and me simply don't get on, never have and never will. I had spoken to Swoff about getting to the game (he is Villa but a gentleman who commands great respect in our local if you get what I mean). He said Gav and me could follow him to some club in Aston, walking distance from the ground. I visited the Swoff household on the Friday night to make sure everything was kosher and he and his missus (Lil) made me very welcome, (don't have the mince pies). We agreed to meet outside his house at 12 ish on the Saturday and I would follow him down. So, after breakfast at the golf course and a swift in the George, we were off.

We arrived at the club for about quarter to one and watched the Man Utd - West Ham game. The place was full of Villa but there was a true friendly atmosphere, to be fair. After we had sunk 2 or 3 we headed off to the ground with young Swoff. He pointed us in the direction of the away end and went his own way. At the corner of the Witton Lane lies the Aston Hotel (nice establishment!!) and as we approached it I noticed a large gathering of lads on the opposite corner just standing about (always fills you with confidence). Then chanting went up and I realised they were Albion (phew). We found our seats after queuing for the toilet in the worst bogs I have seen in a long time. We were in the corner of the Witton Lane and the North Stand with Villa above us (allegedly). Last time I was here we lost 4 - 0 in an embarrassing cup-tie, the time before I was playing right midfield for the school in the all-Birmingham schools final. Villa Park is a special stadium for its obvious history and for the school boy memories I have of the place (twice I played there) but it is the fact that it is Villa, claret and bloody blue that gives you that strange feeling. You know, the one that is similar to never forgetting something you don't like. Have you ever thought that you can remember even the most acute detail about an experience you didn't enjoy or you have the ability to recall irrelevant facts about something that you hate? Well, this is true for me and this place.

Seeing the famous blue and white stripes come out the tunnel at Villa Park brought a tingle to my spine, the hairs stood up as I tried to clap my heroes. The game started with them being comfortably on top. They passed far better than us and I thought we were in for a tatering. Things didn't get any better, when after a foul, Roberts decided to mouth off for a while so the ref. booked him for dissent and promptly moved the ball 10 yards closer to our goal - nice. Somebody hammered it against the wall and it broke really unfortunately into the path of England wannabe Vassell (lucky bleeders) who put the Vile 1 up after about 15mins. Gutted. The last thing you want to see is them "gets" above you laughing and chanting in your face. On the question of support, I feel it necessary to point out that before the visit of the Albion, Villa's average home attendance was hovering around the 30,000 mark. The attendance for the game was announced at around 41,000 which just leaves me to ask the question, where have you been all season Villa? It is also fair to say that for the first time this season we were perfectly correct to sing "You're only here 'cause it's Albion".

The goal seemed to liven the Albion up and we started to play a bit. Koumas again stood out in the middle of the park as play maker and creative spark. He was skipping past people and making things happen. On about the half-hour mark the ball broke to him on the edge of the box and he instinctively side footed it into the bottom corner in front of the Albion. 1 - 1. Now I have celebrated some goals in my time - Wembley '93, Molineux loads of times, Palace in May but a goal at Villa Park is something else. I went berserk. Like a man completely out of control I was on the stairs out of our row jumping, shouting, gesturing and generally looking totally barmy for about 2 minutes. I was so exhausted I thought I was going to pass out by the time the fans had settled again. I glanced up at the so-called Villa section above us in the Witton Lane and saw pockets of fans jumping around all over the place - Albion everywhere! The police and stewards couldn't eject them from the ground because there was simply too many of them. All week I heard stories of Albion fans being in the Villa sections in all areas of the ground. Big club Villa, couldn't sell their tickets, mind.

The next hour saw Villa the better side to be fair but Hoult was on England form again. As the game got scrappy, old man Staunton was red carded for an elbow on Dichio, which sent a shiver down my spine - we never beat ten men. Loads of Villa fans made for the exit on 90 mins, that was that, another point for the Albion and 2 dropped I suppose for them. Then 2 minutes into injury time someone rammed a knife into my heart. Well not exactly, but I imagine the pain to be similar to that which I felt when some German bloke in midfield for them hit a speculative shot that took a decisive deflection with the ball rocketing into the top corner. Time seemed to stand still, I watched the ball in slow motion, there was no noise, my heart stopped beating, then the net bulged and the roars went up. The mood amongst the Albion fans was as though somebody had died, no joke. I think it was me. I stared in disbelief simply unable to speak. Gav and me trudged for the exit and the night sky. To say I was gutted is too simple and obvious here. I actually felt numb with shock and sick in my stomach. Liverpool fans know what I am on about - remember being one nil up at Old Trafford in the Cup before letting in 2 in the last minute? Remember when Waddle missed against the Germans from the spot in 1990? Exactly. Gav and me exchanged few words as I drove home through Handsworth and Winson Green. I was not looking forward to the pub that night because I knew every plastic Villa fan in Oldbury would miraculously appear from nowhere to take the piss. True to form, Viney, Jacko, etc. all managed to say a few words to me that night, I wouldn't mind but the last time Jacko went to Villa Park John Gidman got the winner!

The bigger picture says we are in deep trouble. Albion are simply not picking up points which means we are odds on favourites for the drop. I just hope it is not all over by the end of February and we become a patronised joke.

Sunderland home

Now if ever there was a six-pointer, this was it. And this was the day to do it. We were obviously playing Sunderland and West Ham were playing Bolton. Bottom four battling it out together.

Albion started the day third from bottom, two points behind the Black Cats and Leeds. A win here would set us up nicely for the visit of that struggling Conference side Arsenal or are they "the awesome defending champions"….?

A quick one in The George with the Smith twins before the usual 2 o'clock pick-up. Tom Ross with the pre-match entertainment on Xtra AM and everyone generally expecting a win. Dichio is partnered up front with Roberts with the rest of the Albion team remaining unchanged for what seems to have been forever. Not the prettiest of starts but then again we are half way through the longest relegation battle in history which started in May (thank you Mr. Marsh) and could well finish by about 11th Jan (Man U at home)!

A minute's silence was held for the remembrance of Sir Bert Millichip, Alan Ashman and Arthur Rowley before today's game and, quite rightly, you could have heard a pin drop!! Both sets of supporters silent in thought before breaking out into song after song all game, creating a tremendous atmosphere.

Phillips and Flo are a real handful for the first five minutes but then, a bit of Albion pressure from two, three, or four corners, I dunno…. but we seemed to have a lot of them.

Dichio was proving a real handful in the air, and the Black Cat's defence must have been relieved to see a Johnson 30-yarder, from a Dichio knockdown, turned away at the last minute by the Sunderland keeper. Then another corner from Koumas manages to sail along the front of the goal where only a touch was needed for a certain goal. Another corner, see what I mean, but this time the pressure pays off as Dichio powered the ball into the back of the net with one of his trade-mark headers.

Boing Boing… Boing Boing… Boing Boing…

Sunderland now completely switched off and the Albion slowly started to take notice of this.

A Clement free kick just clears the bar and then Jason Koumas guides a more central free kick in the right hand side of the net. That's better Albion. Another goal please....

Well five minutes later, just after the half hour mark, Roberts is brought down during one of his runs and from the resulting free-kick, Koumas guides the ball up over the wall and past the outstretched arms of Jurgen Macho. Excellent! Fantastic! Bravo! Much-o Boing-io!

A slight scare in the last few minutes of the first half when Igor's back pass was a little too short. Flo intercepted, rounded Hoult but Michael Gray came charging in and blazed the ball over the bar when a goal looked odds-on.

Second half started well, Roberts' surging run found Balis on the overlap but his indecision meant the ball sailed harmlessly over the bar!

Now at this point everything is going O.K. but from now on it all goes a bit Pete Tong, a bit pear-shaped, a "right balls up" is how some might describe it! I'll try and explain, even though it is really shit!

A harmless Sunderland hoof forward is completely misjudged by Gregan, Phillips is in like shot and before anyone had time to recover, the ball is nestling in the bottom corner! Sort it out Sean!!!!!!!!!!!!!

Moore then blocks a shot on the edge of the Baggies box, which would have been goal-bound. Then from out on the left wing, Phillips comes dancing across with the ball. Put your foot in Igor... past Igor. Kick him Siggy.... past Siggy... Guess what?

See previous goal... Ball nestling in the corner of the net!!!! From then on, Sunderland should have taken all three points. A quick free-kick flashes across Russell Hoult and away to safety and then Hoult produces some heroics with a save from a 25 yard shot from McCann.

The only real shots on target from Albion in the second half were a couple of wild efforts from Johnson and a tame left-footer from Koumas... I told you it was shit!

Unbelievable. How can you throw away a 2-goal lead at home to a Sunderland side that is destined to go down and so low on confidence they may as well each hold a white flag when they run out? Gutted, to say the least. Albion, what are you doing to me? It is times like this that you genuinely ask yourself whether it is all worth it.

Arsenal home

Boxing Day and the visit of the Champions. As Albion are looking more and more likely to play Division One football next year, the last thing we wanted was to play the cream of English football in front of a sell out crowd and on TV. Arsenal have never been a fancied team, have they? They have never captured the neutrals' hearts like Liverpool did in the 80s and Man Utd did (I think) in the 90s. It is very difficult to feel much for what is basically a foreign legion of world (French) stars managed by a seemingly characterless Frenchman who looks like the nasty boss off The Simpsons. Arsenal are popular in and around London and with the tabloids, the odd Cockney TV celebrity (usually B status), Frank McKlintock and the entire population of French North Africa. There's something about a supporter of Arsenal - you know, you can spot them a mile off. Me and my mates often play that game. You see someone on the telly, in the street or pub and guess their team. Needless to say it is rarely West Brom. By us, the "supporters" of Liverpool, Man Utd and now Arsenal more recently are so easy to spot it's no fun playing anymore. I don't know what it is but there's something that gives them away. Perhaps it is the fact that more often than not they are happy or is it their obvious supply of cash? Or simply the fact that they discuss the game in great detail when you know they haven't been anywhere near the ground in their life, (sorry they went on an organised tour some years ago).

We needed 3 points desperately but lets face it we were not going to get them against Arsenal. At the Library earlier in the season they battered us with a 5-goal display that could have been 10 to be fair. It is my opinion that Arsenal will win the league again this season because Liverpool and Man Utd are simply not in their class at the moment. With these thoughts in mind I headed for the Hawthorns believing a 4 or 5 goal defeat was seriously on the cards. The atmosphere was great again inside the ground. Makes me worry about next season with the visit of Grimsby etc. and their 50 fans or so!! Arsenal played in their change strip of gold (for God's sake, I ask you, gold!) and fielded a very strong side that included World

Cup winners Henry, Wiltord and Vieira with England quartet Seaman, Cole, Keown (animal) and Campbell. The other 4 were made up from internationals from different countries around the globe (so was the bench). To be fair, on paper it was men against boys even if these "men" did TV adverts for all sorts of products and dressed like catwalk stars on a daily basis.

On 3 minutes the unthinkable happened. Corner from the left (as I look at it) and Dichio rose like a salmon to plant a superb header past the pony tailed England Number 2. I nearly wrote Dichio rose and Seaman was all over the place but I don't think my mom would be too happy with that! One nil to the Albion - you must be joking? The place erupted. I jumped like a nutter in a bear hug with the bloke next to me (only done that twice even though I have sat next to him for 4 years I think!). Boing Boing the whole ground bounced to a rhythmic Baggie beat - a fantastic sight to be fair. I think it was the shock of scoring against the Champions and so early that took the Albion fans by surprise because we went wild and sang our hearts out on all sides for the next 10 minutes. The "Golden Boys" didn't know what had hit them. Even their manager (the late Helen Daniels of Neighbours fame) was at the edge of his technical area. Have that you Cockney ...." was the gist of things for the next few minutes. The rest of the half was a little give and take without really threatening again but I was happy to hear the half time whistle go, to be fair. In a strange way, I just knew Arsenal would come out and really go for it in the second half and they did. 2 mins in and Jeffers latched onto a slightly deflected through ball to equalise. Shit. We have another 43mins plus stoppages to hold on against the free scoring Champions. The next 15mins were going to be crucial. They had a lot of possession and moved like well-organised Red Arrow pilots for what seemed like an eternity. I genuinely thought they were going to get 2 or 3 more and really rub our noses in it. I waited and waited but it never came. With ten minutes to go Roberts, who incidentally was fouled in this match as often as he has been all season without any protection from gutless, one-eyed refs. left the animal Keown (who still hasn't received any punishment for his GBH on Van Nistlerooy) for dead and hammered a shot that beat speedy Seaman only to hit the inside of the post and rebound to safety. Lucky side the Albion you know. Then with 3 minutes to go we cleared the ball only for it to hit another Albion defender and bounce straight into Henry's path in front of goal. More good fortune for the Albion!! He promptly rounded Hoult and efficiently slid the ball into the empty net. 2 - 1, all over, lost again. I think I could have cried because even though you never back the Albion ever, I just could not see Arsenal scoring. They did not impress me at all. The reports afterwards in the London press were nothing short of ridiculous. One comic actually wrote that Arsenal were back to Championship winning form in a column that only mentioned the Albion by name once. By reading it you could have been forgiven for thinking "The Arsenal" had been the only team playing out there.

Oh well lost again, relegation looms large. The ghost of Christmas past and present had paid us a visit this Boxing Day afternoon. The worry is though, was it the ghost of Christmas yet to come?

Charlton away

Can I, first of all, say that if I thought the Everton view was bad, this comes a close second? A steel girder is blocking my view of the far right hand corner of the pitch and the right hand post of the near goal. Therefore if the names of corner takers are missing and I don't say who is on front/back post, please forgive me.

A nice early start accompanied another hangover during the Christmas festivities. I know that Terry, Stef, and myself are now familiar with the route to Dover (that's another story!!!), but this journey seemed to take just as long. Down the M1, round the M25, Dartford Tunnel (bridge) and all that. Then drive nearly all the way into London. Literally a stones-throw from the Dome.

Few drinks in Antigalllicanallyable or something. This place looked like it was going to break out into a cock-fighting arena – and I'm not talking about the Albion fans! Big open room seating at either end on raised platforms, pool table in the middle with the biggest slab of wood (can you have slabs of wood?) on top and everyone standing around watching a nature program on the TV. "Someone put the footy on, will you?!" Short walk to the ground, which looks quite impressive except for the away end. Typical!!

Forgot to mention; for today's game, not only will we be away from the Smith twins, but all five of us (Andy's mate from work came as well) are sitting apart. Picked tickets on way down so no arguing when we get there. When we get to our seats, we find out that we're quite close to each other anyway – which was nice.

Game started and straight away Charlton were putting pressure on us…Oh no, not again. Two fine saves from Hoult and then chaos in the area and he saves the day again. Another corner….Shit, one nil! Free header straight through the arms of Hoult! Come on Albion…

From then on it was as if Charlton had been told they couldn't go in our area again. All Albion….honestly. Koumas and Johnson winning everything in midfield. Roberts getting fouled EVERY time he got the ball and still not getting the free kicks he deserved. And then HE gets booked for constantly moaning – well if your black and blue all over you're going to shout out at some point!

Roberts has a shot blocked from close range by the keeper, Koumas hits the post from a free-kick, their keeper makes a few more excellent saves, Johnson does his usual over the bar efforts and their defenders clear a few off the line. Not a bad first half really. If only the ball would go in the back of the net. Can we have a bit of luck second half please and "Oi ref! Open your eyes a bit more!?" Well second half started much the same as the first half ended. Not much from Charlton and chances galore for Albion. Big Dave had a few chances, Dichio, Roberts, AJ. They were all having a go. Then Roberts twists and turns into the area to be brought down be Rufus. Such an obvious penalty and Steve "fat green git" Dunn gives nothing!!!!!! Is it an unwritten rule for newcomers to the Premier League not to have any decisions go in their favour?

Towards the end of the half Megson decides to throw on Dobie for Chambers and then he brings on Hughes for Koumas. WHAT?? Take off bloody Wallwork instead – he is soooo slow! Anyway we leave with a few minutes to go but manage to see Dobie hit the bar from 20 yards as we battle through the crowds. You can imagine what they will say on radio and TV, another battling performance by the Baggies – if they continue like this they won't go down!

Yes we will – we're not getting any points!!!!!!!!!!!!!

Fulham away

We got to Birchley Island and Smithy got the call from his Dad - match is off. It was about quarter to ten which is not too bad but don't forget, this was New Years Day!! What a bummer. January the 1st has got to be the worst day of the year, the most forgettable time of anyone's life, right? No cash, headache, freezing cold, Cilla Black on TV (not for much longer yippee), nobody coming out to play, the smell of drink makes you heave, etc. Add to that, the footy being cancelled and well, you may as well go back to bed and get up in 3 days time. Fulham, that huge club from the metropolis, that a non-British passport holder is toying with for the moment, have not got their own ground as I speak. They are currently looking to build a new stadium by 2004. I would think a capacity of 20000 should do it or even 10000, for when Mr Al fayed gets bored with his plaything and pulls the plug on it and Fulham return to their real selves. They play at Loftus Road, home of QPR but the pitch couldn't take another game as it is not getting any "rest" and the SE have had a downpour for a prolonged period recently. We went to McDonalds at Birchley - sorry no Breakfasts so drove to Sava - no can do, we went to the one by the Bass House (you know where I mean) - same story. So here I was 10am New Years Day morning eating a hamburger in McDonalds thinking of the day ahead - what a life!

Man Utd home

I don't care what anyone says the fixture every fan looks for each year is Man Utd at home. Love 'em or hate 'em they are this country's premier club. Sorry Liverpool your days were in a different decade and Arsenal, well you are yet to have yours but there is something about a London club that makes me think you never will. More fans than any other football team in the world. More fans in Malaysia than in Manchester. A higher turnover than a number of small African economies and more silverware in our recent memory than the Antiques Roadshow, Manchester United Football Club. Truth is, those that hate, do so out of envy and in response to over representation in the Media. It is true, human nature leads you to dislike the same things too often - Cilla Black, Carol Vorderman, Bryan Adams' number one after 17 bloody weeks, etc. So when Man Utd are on the TV again and have three pages of sports coverage in any one of ten Dailies, is it any wonder the British public, in some cases, take an instant dislike to them? Strangely though, for some, it is not a dislike but hatred. Man City and Liverpool I can appreciate but if you were to do a poll for your club to see who was hated most, other than local rivals, MUFC would be top. It doesn't stop there either. Not just the club, but all playing staff, past and present are disliked, fans are hated and in particular those that live outside the Manchester area. I for one, have always admired United and well, to be honest I have a soft spot for them (all right calm down). My theory is I have watched live football outside the top division for 95% of my life (since I could go up alone) and have therefore, had no direct contact with Man Utd as an Albion fan. Second factor is, although I do not see myself as a football purist I did get hooked on the team of the early to mid nineties when at university (Albion were playing Peterborough etc.). This is when Giggs, Sharpe, Cantona, etc. strutted around the park with a flair I had never seen before. Third and final factor is probably the most important of all - my natural feeling towards them has always been positive. I don't believe in second teams or any of that nonsense but if I had one, it would be them!

1-0 to the Albion, 30 seconds later, 1-1!!

Now I don't know whether I should include this next bit but I believe that if I am as honest as possible it may sound better when read (you idiot). The missus loves David Beckham. There, I've said it. Now before I go any further, it must be said here that Fay is not one of these women at football that does your head in. You know, the ones who actually sing for Gods sake and make comments about the players or tactics. This makes me sound like a chauvinistic pig I know but I promise you I am not. It is just once again a natural feeling I have towards a girl talking about football, sorry. Fay is far cuter than that. She knows what is acceptable because she says the same to me when she hears other women making daft comments. (Can't believe I've written that paragraph). Anyway, Beckham - again, love him (the Wife) or hate him (all those that drink in the Bar and forget he is England's best player and most consistent over the last 2 years). Fay wanted to get there early. This could seriously upset the Saturday morning drinking routine on match days at home but, as we may never see him again at the Hawthorns (in the League), I thought it was fair enough. We got there just before 2pm - a record for the last 10 years. Fay spent the next half an hour towards the front of the Smethwick hoping to catch a glimpse of Golden Locks. Loads of children were at the front of all 4 stands shouting his name; he gave a wave and a smile occasionally. Say what you like about him but boy does he create a stir like no other and I mean no other, not since Georgie the Belfast Boy. Cameras have very rarely been taken into the Hawthorns unless they were owned by Central TV but whenever they had a corner, loads of flashlights went off - unbelievable! I know what you are thinking "Ponse, Puff", etc. any derogatory remark but on that field nobody gave more than Beckham and you know what? Nobody ever does. People around me shouted insults towards him just for the shear hell of it because for some it is "fun" to abuse the "different" one, the one that stands out, the easy target, I mean did you see what it said in the Daily Star? I just felt content that a true world star was playing on my home pitch and I loved every minute of it. What was the point in trying to spoil a once in a life time opportunity with blind hatred? We have been accustomed to teams fielding 11 players of which 9 sometimes 10 have been unheard of. Is that what you would prefer? Thought not. The majority of United players got similar treatment and I know it's a case of what do you expect but my God, how I wished just one of them was in blue and white stripes.

The game itself was a forgettable experience for the Albion, we never really had any control. Koumas did, however, do the unthinkable when he ran with the ball directly towards Barthez's goal and hammered a shot inside the right hand upright. 1 - 0 nil to the Albion - you are joking, right? We went barmy. I was still celebrating when Van Nistlerooy was turning away with his arm in the air saluting his equaliser! Yes that's right we held onto the lead for less than a minute. Clement miscontrolled and Beckham crossed for VN to poke through Hoult's legs. Great, you score against the biggest club in Britain and don't even have the chance to take it in. This was the turning point make no mistake. They had got back to level terms without having to panic or argue or be concerned about being one down. Only one result now - United at a canter and so it proved. My beloved Baggies were outplayed and classed by a far superior side. This is a team with a 100% record in the Champions League with players worth over 200 million pounds. I was as gutted as the next man because remove the "isn't it a lovely day for the Albion?" and you still see us at the bottom of the league staring relegation in the face. Even taking this into account I still thought it a little ridiculous and over the top for some fans to berate the players and demand so much more from what is basically a reasonably good first division side. I heard some astonishing quotes like "You only have to get stuck in" and "Too much respect" added to "Pass and move, that's all you have to do" and I thought am I hearing this right?

I was so happy to see my heroes run out with a team of world superstars led by Roy Keane. It may seem small time and a bit namby-pamby but remember it has been 16 years since we played anyone of any value and lets face it, the game has moved on at a geometric rate since then. We finished the day bottom of the table as West Ham got a point at home to Newcastle. I reflected on a one off occasion (soon to be confirmed) and Fay went home, only slightly peeved that in the whole 90 minutes they didn't get one corner in front of the Smethwick End!

Leeds United away

It's starting to feel like the start of the season again. Man Utd then Leeds. Having lost to Man U again, hopefully we can stop a trend setting in by taking some, if not all of the points from our trip to Elland Road.

We were all over them for the first 30 minutes at home and then Bowyer destroyed us in the second half. He's now at West Ham, so you never know!!

New route to the North – A38 thank you Mr. Smith – far too many road works on the M6/M42 these days!

Arrived in this Industrial Estate in the shadows of the ground on the other side of the M62 at about mid-day after the now traditional Big Big Breakfast from RoadChef. We've got instructions from a Blue Nose – sorry Birmingham City fan – from Stef's school, who knows where to have a drink "2 minutes from the ground"! This could be good!

Well, I take it all back. There it is, the Magic Sponge Bar (and Bowling). Unfortunately, we have to gatecrash a kiddie's party but never mind! Man Utd on Sky again!! Very short walk to the ground. Burgers, programmes, toilets, seats.
Hooray, at last. This is the first time all of us have sat together for an away game. Not bad considering we're half way through the season!

The game itself is a scrappy affair. Not that many clear cut chances really. Hoult produced some outstanding saves from Smith in particular. Talking of saves, you'd have thought that with Mr. Seamen on his last legs, Sven Goran Erikkson would have been at this game to watch the performances of Robinson and Hoult. Well I would have, if I were him.

Good saves from Albion's keeper kept out shots from Bakke, Kewel and Viduka before the save of the day prevented Smith opening the scoring. At the other end Dobie should have done better after beating the Leeds back four, and from substitute Wallwork's cross an outstretched foot would have been 1-0 to the Baggies. Dobie was playing due to the suspension of Roberts from his "mouthy" bookings!!

With nothing really happening at either end in the second half, Megson brought on Hughes after an hour. Hughes managed to liven things up a little, but after earlier treatment Viduka was grounded again by a challenge from Johnson. Not a wild challenge but unnecessary all the same. Yellow Card. Three minutes later, Radebe handles a through ball for Hughes to run onto, in the area. Penalty. Yes. Three points.

NO! Uriah Rennie gives a free kick to Leeds for a push by Hughes! Is he blind? Hughes is incensed. The Albion players are annoyed. Johnson says a bit too much. Red Card. Johnson…idiot. Uriah Rennie…you can guess what he was called! The bloke next to Dave Price (our chauffeur for the day) was pretending to shoot Mr. Rennie. I don't think we need to go that far – some of the other refs perhaps. Come on lads. Only fifteen minutes or so left…

We're nearly celebrating a goal with only minutes on the clock when Wallwork makes Robinson show what he's worth. Unfortunately, he manages to tip the 20-yard effort just over the bar. Never mind. You can't complain at a draw away at Leeds. We should have had the three points but they did create more chances, even if they weren't better chances if you know what I mean.

It's becoming a bit of a tradition to listen to Talk Sport on the journey home but I normally fall asleep (if I'm not driving, ha ha). However, Adrian Durham – I think that's his name – has got it in for the Albion lately. He's so negative towards us and there's Lawrie McMenemy trying his best to defend us. One caller, an Albion fan who was at the game, was discussing the penalty incident and Mr. Durham replied saying "Well, you have to actually get into the area to get a penalty these days!" Cheeky sod! We've been denied more penalties than we've given away. Doesn't he watch The Premiership? Oh no, of course not. Peterborough wouldn't be on!

Watford v W B A 25th January 2003 FA Cup 4th Round

Well, what can I say? If you were there you'll know exactly what I mean! No passion, definitely no ideas when we had the ball long enough to try something. No corners until the last few minutes, Watford passing it much, much, much better. You'd have thought they were the Premiership side – not that that label means anything!

Dad has only been to one or two games recently; the last time he watched the Albion was in the 70's! He's indoctrinated by it at the moment though, Mom got him a ticket – "We'll all go!" she said.

Don't think he'll bother volunteering himself for another "day out"!

I think the only real way to describe the formation is:

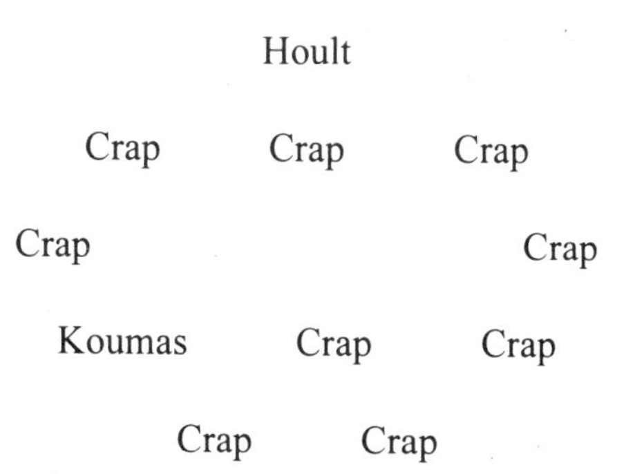

You get the picture?! I don't think Mr. Megson was too happy either. I'll leave the last words to him:

"....that's the first time for two and a half years they've been booed off the pitch......"

Charlton home

Midweek, minus God knows what with the wind chill, just after the Watford FA Cup debacle and bottom of the league. This is what was at the forefront of my mind as we approached the ground for our home game with the mighty Charlton Athletic. Now one thing has always amazed me over the years - how the hell have Charlton survived in the top flight? Their support is poor, financial backing lacking and history, devoid of honours. The away following from SE London was crap to say the least, if there was 200 fans then that's all there was. Their team was packed with steady pros, no superstars and little on the bench - how do they stay up year after year?

Megson had been saying in the week that our performance against First Division Watford was unacceptable. He singled out 2 players (Hoult and Koumas) that had bothered to try and slated the rest. Listening closely to him and reading his words in the local press, started me wondering. I got the impression he was losing faith in the team and maybe believed himself that the Premier was too much for us at this stage. If he did he was not wrong. Albion are not a top flight outfit. The team playing week in week out is a reasonably good First Division team. The squad of 16 - 18 pros is very poor by Premier League standards. The Board has little inclination in resolving this imbalance as at the time of writing, there is one day left in the mid season transfer window and we have managed to secure the services of an unknown Nigerian full back. That, in itself, says volumes for West Bromwich Albion Football Club. Don't forget, we are bottom of the league with the weakest squad in the Division by far and are desperate for a striker, centre-half and 2 full backs. We have been "linked" with (incidentally, I hate that term in the press because it usually means absolutely nothing) 5 or 6 players who for one reason or another have said NO to playing for the Albion. I mean what does it tell you when a Spanish centre half chooses to retire early, rather than play for us and Tim Sherwood would rather drop down a division to play for Portsmouth?! It's not as if we are skint. Gate receipts must be through the roof and TV money etc. has still not been spent. Don't get me wrong I am not one of these idiots who want us to spend spend spend and end up like Leicester, Derby, Coventry, Bradford, etc. but surely 5 or 6 million on 3 players is not too much to ask of a so called Premier League club with ambitions of staying in the division is it? It really annoys me sometimes - different men, same board at the Albion. To make matters worse the Blues, who for the best part (95%) of their history have always looked up to the Albion in terms of trophies, history, support, etc. are spending freely. I even hear that they "want Albion to stay up" and "isn't it a shame". Patronised by Blues supporters, that's how poor things have become!

The match itself lived up to expectations - dull, drab, dreary, poor quality, etc. pick any one you want. The crowd, who have been magnificent this season, not like the so called aristocrats from Aston and the ridiculously impatient Dingles reached a brick wall against Charlton. It could turn out to be a watershed for the season. Apart from a few half-hearted chants it was mainly criticism and expletives. Clement wasn't playing so he missed his torrent of abuse but Jason Roberts was told to sod off back down the lower leagues (he might as well stay with us then) and AJ was instructed to take a rest (for whom exactly?). Most of the players got some stick and even the Lord of the Manor was politely asked to vacate his post by one bloke! I had an awful flash back - G Harby was left back, Stacey North was preparing to take a throw in, Paul Williams was calling for it back stick, Dave Gilbert was out of breath and Crichton was shouting leave it. Bobby Gould was giving the instructions from the bench. Yes it reminded me of those dark days - days, when saying you were an Albion fan was a genuine rib tickler. I panicked. Would we get another a point? Are all of our half-decent players going to leave? Crowds back to the 15 000 mark and worst of all, the atmosphere at the ground back to one of despair, silence and non-stop criticism.

For the record, we hit the post, squandered 2 very good chances (not AJ again, surely?) had 2 penalty appeals waved away (Andy Durso - say no more) and forced Kiely into one world class save. Now I know what you are thinking and yes, you are right - we didn't score. Charlton had one chance that Lisbie headed in off Dichio. Lost 1 - 0. Some things in football are set in stone. I believe one of them is "If Charlton do the double over you, you are going down". Need I say more? Booed off for the second time in 5 days, West Ham scored a last minute winner, Man City thump Fulham 4, sign Robbie Fowler for 6 million and play us Saturday. I love the Albion like I don't know what but the thought of spending the next 10 - 15 games or so watching abject performances for a lot of money (I'm getting married in August and the new house is like a building site) does not fill me with much joy. And yes, if you are wondering, the Premier League thing has well and truly worn off and the realisation of Nationwide football with Rotherham, Grimsby and Walsall etc. is now nudging itself ever closer.

Man City away

Well, after last year's 4 points out of 6 against the blue half of Manchester, the home tie of this season's fixture had been a bit poor to say the least! Maybe the away tie would be somewhat better… Oh no, perhaps not, they've just signed Robbie Fowler!! He will definitely score… and Anelka will… and that bloody Goat-bloke will if he gets a chance!

We haven't been on the M5 for more than sixty seconds and car predictions are already in full swing! Paul 3-0 City; Stef 5-0 City; Andy 4-0 City; Rich 1-1; Gav "2-1 Albion and a man sent off?" the others cry… no 2-1 City with a man sent off! Not even at Oldbury turn-off and we've already conceded defeat! M5, M6, and M56… we're getting good at this now.

Slightly lost around the outskirts of Manchester, but directions from a petrol station attendant soon put us back on track. Right at lights, past the Hospital, left at lights, straight over then on left. Oh yeah, there it is. "I thought I could see a stand across there before" "No you couldn't – shut up!!" Park up and head for The Sherwood which Grorty Dick and the Internet Away Guide describe as the home pub! What are we doing?! This place is a dive, a shit hole, and a ruff arse effort of a pub but as it's only 12:15 there's no one else there except a few eager Albion fans. We "take" the far side of the pub and wait our turn for the pool table. "Last game, please folks!" Covers on – no pool!

To liven things up just that little more we decide to go quids-in for first goal scorer. Can't really remember who had who, but they were the obvious Anelka, Fowler, Roberts, type suggestions. And to REALLY make the afternoon more bearable we decide to chip in again, two quid each this time, for that old World Cup favourite – Corners. Basically, somebody starts with a tenner and every time there is a corner you pass the tenner on. Whoever has it at the final whistle keeps it! Can get quite exciting with two minutes to go I can tell you. Gamble, gamble, gamble. But you could say watching the Albion week in week out is a gamble!

The game starts, as you'd expect with all the expectation on the strike force of Anelka and Fowler. Enter Gilchrist, Moore and Gregan to spoil the show… for the city fans anyway! Clement was the first to make either keeper do any real work, when from a right sided Koumas cross, his powerful header was saved by Nash's feet. Only a few Minutes later almost a mirror image. Free kick on the left swung in by Koumas and Clement gets up highest to connect with the ball and head it over the line. Brilliant, absolutely brilliant! But hold on; CLEMENT first goal scorer, nobody picked him! Probably due to the fact that we didn't think he would be playing! That doesn't matter though, one – nil Albion. Get in there!

We're getting quite used to this now, ahead against City, United the other week, Arsenal on Boxing Day. But alas, again, as per usual, we can't hold on to the lead for very long! Four minutes this time, cross comes in, an attempted header from Foe is enough to distract Gilchrist enough to lose bearings and glance a header right into the bottom corner – of our net unfortunately!!

Not a lot to report after that, in the first half but overall, a much better Albion performance. And as I said earlier, Gregan Moore and Gilchrist spoiling the Man City show.

Second half continued in much the same vein. Not so much as constant pressure from either side but when chances arrived they failed to make them count.

I really find it hard to say, but credit where credit's due, Wallwork and McInnes were instrumental in midfield. Winning tackles, keeping possession, creating moves and generally allowing Koumas to break forward whenever he could to start another attack. This was all very encouraging and the fans responded in full vocal backing. Again, Albion appeared to have sold out of their away ticket allocation. It looks like they've had to bring in some Lego stands in the corners to provide seats for the fans but apparently they are permanent fixtures. Wouldn't like to be sitting there in the rain!! No roofs!!

Dichio came on for a tired looking Hughes and he seemed to liven up the Baggies a little. Roberts and Dichio do seem to link up well but the ball either gets trapped between Roberts' feet or he tries too hard when he should really play the simple ball more often.

Half way through the half, Albion have a bit more pressure on the Man City area. A few corners and free kicks awarded and then from a free kick on the right, Clement flicked the ball on at the near post, Roberts helped it a little further and then Big Dave stroked it home at the far post. Get in there!!

Boing Boing!! Boing Boing!! Boing Boing!! Boing Boing!! Boing Boing!! Boing Boing!! Boing Boing!! Boing Boing!!

Where's your lipstick Rodney Marsh?? Etc etc etc. As you can imagine, we were going crazy!! Moms and Dads, Aunts and Uncles, Brothers and Sisters… well me and my cousin anyway!! Come on now, only fifteen or so minutes to hold on.

Then Neil Barry awards Albion a free kick on the half way line. Can't really remember what it was for but suddenly all eyes turned to the edge of the Man City penalty area. Sommeil, the City central defender, was lying on the floor, Jason Roberts was leaning over him, and the linesman on the far side was waving his flag like there was no tomorrow! No one really knew what had happened, but after a quick consultation, out came the red card!! A closer inspection on The Premiership is definitely needed!

Now can we just recall the predictions? For once, I would have been right. Two – one Albion with a man sent off. All this Robbie Fowler nonsense had put me off. He wouldn't have scored "if he'd have played all night"!

Anyway, final whistle goes after a few slight scares but a thoroughly deserved three points. Now, I don't know if the Police were actually keeping us in, or we were just a bit excited, but we were still "Boinging" when the players came back out for their "warm down". What a stupid sounding term that is. Oh, this takes me back to those hazy days at the Stadium of Light. When was it? Yes, that's right, last year!!!!

Players back in, time to go. We're still singing as we head for the gates. Now the story really starts!! As we get outside, everything changes. Police everywhere. Horses, vans, can't hear any dogs but they must be somewhere! Groups of lads everywhere. Can't really tell who is supporting who! Very moody!

As we turn corner after corner, trying to make our way in the direction of the car, we are faced with groups of lads lurking on corners, individuals standing in the middle of the road looking all ‘ard with they’re Rockport boots, denim jeans, Timberland jackets and the increasingly popular Burberry checkered caps. You can spot hooligans a mile off these days; unfortunately they don’t hit you these days, they stab you with whatever they can get their hands on. Walking through groups of lads all up for it is not a pleasant experience. I heard one Manc call his boys and direct them through the alleyways and houses on Moss Side saying they could meet 'em down here. The smell of stale beer, hatred and the violence to follow has a heart pounding effect. I genuinely felt sick as we walked past the mob and had to mingle with them on the way to our car. We didn't speak, kept our eyes on the ground and walked swiftly trying not to stand out. Before the police arrived I thought we were in for a hiding. I would consider myself a people's person, one who can communicate in many situations and my last act of violence was in second year as a 13year old boy. This counts for nothing, however, when faced with irrational behaviour from half drunk, adrenaline-pumped idiots intent on smashing your face in. I sometimes wished I didn't think as much as I do because only God knows what went through my mind as we walked that walk! In a strange way we all started laughing with the car in sight, a release of tension and the sign of relief I suppose that we had successfully negotiated the gauntlet of City fans, thanks mainly to a rather large white Police horse. Now, I seem to remember one of those several years ago…

As we approach the car I think Andy’s mate Rich best summed it all up: “I was f***ing shitting myself!!”

Says it all really. Bring on Bolton!

Bolton home

Real 6 pointer this one! Stupid statement when you think about it that. Nevermind, I can see what people mean - they are 5 or 6 points above us and only a couple of places away from the relegation zone, the last place of which is occupied by us! Not the most glamorous of fixtures really but I suppose most teams say the same about the "famous" blue and white stripes.

They controlled the first 20 minutes if I'm honest. They passed and moved and looked as though they were going to run us ragged. Midfield was non-existent. Ronnie Stalwart (Wallwork) is too slow and McInnes is well, not a Premiership midfielder. Then it happened, the worse possible start for the Albion - someone had a relatively tame shot that bounced just in front of England's No. 1. He made a mess of it, to be fair and palmed the ball out to Petterson, I think his name is, (Bolton are full of foreigners, never mind Chelsea!) who promptly put the other "Wanderers" one up. Great, Bolton are 5 points ahead of us but we have a game in hand (Yeah so?). If we beat them and win our game in hand, (apparently they have found another red bus at the South Pole) we will be above them - 6 pointer this!! Roberts was again letting himself down - no more frightening runs and no goals for about the 16th game in a row. Fans around me had obviously had enough of this and now began to sound like Dingles. You know what I'm on about, virtually waiting for and maybe wanting Roberts to mess up so they could slate him. Real hatred born out of frustration and anxiety - you know what I mean don't you? Made me think what their reaction would be if he had scored (he didn't and missed a sitter). The rest of the game was mainly Albion in possession without really having that many ideas, although Gregan hit the inside of a post and watched the ball run across the line and Roberts snatched at a volley with the air of a man troubled with confidence. Bolton proceeded to time waste and commit "good" fouls if you understand what I mean (yes you did Sam don't deny it).

At this point I feel it necessary to mention our old friend Mr Ellery. During the first half their foreign keeper (foreign? You're joking) came out of his box and attempted a clearance/tackle. He did neither and fouled Roberts with no other players around. Ellery came running over towards the incident reaching for his back pocket immediately. Now I know this is no guarantee but his approach, body language and general appearance suggested his intent was to send the keeper off. Come on, you've all seen it but no, not the headteacher! Unfortunately, McInnes the idiot, decided to take a quick free kick that was easily cleared off the line and Ellery had his opportunity to do what he does best - nothing, avoid the incident and wave play on. I nearly passed out with rage. The crowd was incensed and let fly with a torrent of abuse aimed at the man in black. The Albion players surrounded him and voiced their opinions too and in the background was Megson going absolutely berserk. Even Ellery had to act this time - he waved a yellow card at the keeper from the half way line in a vain attempt to appease the fans etc. What a joke. He may have got the decision right in hindsight and McInnes certainly didn't help but I swear his initial reaction was to send the keeper off - you clutch to anything and everything at the bottom of the league!

Getting nothing from this game would have not only been an outrageous injustice but it would also have left us with a near impossible task of catching them (or anybody else for that matter). We pushed for the equaliser and the 4th official held up 4 minutes, I think. Free kick to the boys on the edge of their area - Koumas floats it this time and Big Dave gets a vital flick on. The ball goes far post where the on rushing AJ, who hasn't hit a barn door all season, lunges in to slide the ball under their keeper to make it 1 - 1 in injury time. We went barmy! I vented some anger at Allardyce who had obviously told his players to take their time and commit fouls if "necessary" and thanked the heavens for small mercies. This point added, to the amazing 3 gained at Main Road last week meant we now had a slight chance of achieving the impossible. Could we honestly stay up? After everything I have been saying, could the Albion retain their top-flight status after I was convinced we were doomed? Who knows but one thing is for sure, the Blues aren't as cocky as they have been in previous weeks!! What a story that would be - we stay up against all the odds and the free spending Blues go down! Watch this space.

Fulham away

Fulham play at someone else's ground, in front of approximately 15,000 fans every other week, shall we say. They have a wage bill for a ridiculous amount of foreign stars that outweighs their general income by millions. Their very existence lies solely in the hands of an Arab businessman still looking for a passport. Wolfie Smith doesn't support them anymore and neither does Hugh Grant for that matter. Supporting Fulham must be a surreal experience because I genuinely feel the majority of those 15,000 fans are true fans - those that went in the Third Division only 5 years ago but what must they honestly think now? Artificial, plastic, precarious, out of touch - it's your choice. I believe all clubs seem to have a belonging. In debt, away from the Cottage, unrecognisable foreign players, and destiny out of hand is certainly not Fulham's. Like the fact that Arsenal seem insistent on doing all things French, it doesn't enter the fans' minds until something goes wrong. As long as Arsenal are winning things nobody cares they have lost their soul and so by the same score, as long as Fulham remain a reasonably good Premier League side their supporters will not think about the bigger picture.

We should have played this game on New Year's Day as mentioned earlier so it was quite lucky for me that the rearranged fixture fell in half term week. Smithy was driving so we set off at 1.30pm (they booked half days and Gav took the whole day off!!) - if only the Albion knew what people did to support them, aye? After about the 50th Burger King this season we arrived in the capital for about 4ish and headed for the BBC. We parked on a "secure" car park past Loftus Road and the surrounding references to Australia and South Africa, but only after the other Smith decided to have trouble with a parking meter! Andy was over generous in Newcastle, if you remember, but this time brother Paul decided to press for a ticket with only 4 quid in instead of 5 so it expired at 8.30 - at the start of the second half!!

Loftus Road has tradition etc. I suppose but I just could not stop thinking about Halesowen Town and the Grove as I walked past it to reach The Springbok. What a beautiful establishment that is! I had to laugh though, Smithy said it had been given a face lift since he last was in here!! We had a laugh but had to endure the Racing Channel or something, which I'm sorry, is the most boring viewing imaginable. We spiced it up a bit by betting 50p on every race, I won one!! The atmosphere was okay but I couldn't stop looking at a group of lads who came in just after us. All season we have avoided trouble at every ground except the Manchester two. Main Road, the other week, brought to my attention that awful feeling you get when you are around football violence. The smart clothes, baseball caps and mobile phones. The loitering and eerieness that acts as a lull before a storm. With these thoughts fresh in mind, the presence of the group of lads dressed accordingly and on the phone with alarming regularity, did put me a little ill at ease on occasions. I think it is a sixth sense I've got but I suss situations out very quickly. These lads were constantly in and out of the pub and not really drinking - need to stay sober? Perhaps I was totally wrong and as the place filled up their presence was no longer an issue.

We got to our seats in the top tear in good time after seeing Skinner in the toilets. He was sitting on the row behind us alone, next to an unsuspecting fan who must have had the night of his life as Frank joked along with him as the match went on. The first half was a non-event but for Hughes to go clean through only to hit it straight at the keeper. Albion taking the lead is vital if we are to get anything from a game - but for two occasions this season so far when we have gained some points, we have scored first in the match. We matched Fulham for 72mins and could have genuinely won the game. They posed no threat and were in no way superior to us. Then, with about 18mins, left a harmless looking ball was played into our box and we didn't react. 1 - 0 Fulham. I couldn't believe it - the chances of us getting anything now were remote. If we don't score, the pressure on our defence is simply too much because psychologically, the players know if we concede the likelihood of us getting two to win is zero - hasn't happened all year! Now I know we would probably lose the game but I wasn't really prepared for the next 4 minutes. 1 - 0 became 2 - 0 after a wonder free kick from A

Foreigner. Then on 76minutes, 2 - 0 became 3 - 0 thanks to a penalty. We left the ground immediately, along with most of the amazing 3200 travelling Albion fans. I was so shocked I simply laughed for most of the way back to the car. Only relegated teams lose in that manner to a very average side.

What people don't realise is, of the 5 of us who went to Fulham, 4 took time off work just to go. We spent the best part of £200 and got nothing for any of our efforts. No doubt we'll do it again in a fortnight but I am beginning to understand why our mom thinks I have gone mad!!

West Ham home

Well after not getting a mention on the tannoy system for my birthday back in August, thought it would be nice to say "Happy Birthday" to Mom at half-time in today's game. That was before Kate, my girlfriend, was kindly informed by the East Stand reception woman, that they weren't doing announcements any more, from this weekend onwards! Now that's just typical! "You can have it in the program or on the screen for £25", she went on to say… Twenty-five bloody quid! I wouldn't mind, but you can't even see the damn screens!

Anyway enough moaning, that comes later! West Ham at home. Beat them at their ground. We need points. They need points. Proper relegation battle! Come on you Baggies!

Didn't start too well, as usual. Well that was until the seventh minute. Big Dave, back post, beat everyone and the keeper. Hit the inside of the post and fell to a Hammer's defender who hacked it clear. Lucky bastards! Then it all seemed to be a midfield scramble for ages and ages and ages. Hughes always seemed to stray offside and a couple of Koumas free kicks later we were on our feet singing a new rendition of an old classic! To the tune of She'll be coming round the mountain"…….

If James can play for England so can I,
If James can play for England so can I,
If James can play for England,
James can play for England,
James can play for England so can I.

David James is one of those keepers who is never confident when he has to jump and catch the ball. A slight flaw in the job description of a goalkeeper, if you ask me, so Koumas' crosses were either just too high or just in front or behind the Albion front two.

Then Mr. Udeze decided to show us what he can do. Down the left wing, past two players, lovely one-two with Dichio and slotted the ball home past the approaching blond, I mean David James. Unfortunately, the officials decided otherwise for the umpteenth time this season. Apparently Hughes was offside, again, even though he was running away from the West Ham goal and he was on the other side of the area! We'll have to have another look tonight with Des and Ally.

Backwards and forwards, up and down the pitch. Then a goal-line clearance saves Hoult's blushes; he's definitely not going to get an England call up at this rate! Then the miss of the season competition started again. After Giggs' efforts in Europe the other night, it was Trevor Sinclair who took centre stage. Ball comes across, fumbled by Hoult, Sinclair surely. No, he manages to hit the ball at such an angle into the ground that it bounces up over Hoult, hits the bar and out for a goal kick. I'll leave that explanation to the experts!

Then all was forgiven as far as West Ham fans and Sinclair were concerned. Deep into first half injury time, Albion can't seem to clear a ball in the right back position and as Sinclair makes a run across the box, the ball is played in to him and with a quick flick of the left foot the ball is nestling in the far corner of the net. I can't believe it! Last kick of the half, literally!

I don't think I have ever seen so many people, so quiet and virtually all sitting down at half time in the Smethwick End. Not even texting on the phones! I think it's starting to sink in that we're more-than-likely going to be relegated!

As the second half started Glen Roeder decided to make a change. On came Jermaine Defoe and off went the unimpressive Di Canio, much to his annoyance. Oooh, temper, temper Paulo!! Then, YES, a lifeline! Koumas, inch perfect cross; Daniel Dichio, centre of box; James, nowhere!!! YES!! Equalizer. Now come on Albion, we know the second half is always better than the first. And it was, we tackled and chased better. We passed much, much better. We had more possession, more chances, more shots, less to do in defence. A brilliant second half as I just said. Only one slight problem though; David James probably had the best half he's ever played. What a shame Sven Goran Eriksson was watching.

Hughes should have scored, then Dichio had a chance - he should have scored too. I have to admit though, they were decent saves, what he lacks on crosses, he more than makes up for in shot stopping. You should still knock it past the keeper in those one-on-one situations though! Then the fireworks started. Hughes played in Dichio from the right hand side of the box and he calmly slotted the ball past James. About 'effin time! All set for another rendition of Where's your lipstick?

Our survey says.... Not this time. Linesman's flag is up AGAIN! Dichio offside this time - more analysis for Mr. Lynham to sort out. They say your luck evens itself out over the season. I think you can guess my response to that!!

This chance for Albion produced yet another talking point as Repka and James went for each other in a full on, all action, poking, pushing and shouting competition. Teammates were on hand to separate them before they started pulling each other's hair and gouging eyes.

68th minute. Now take note. Remember this, it could prove costly. Les Ferdinand with a free header at the back post. Fortunately, he rattles the bar. Unfortunately, Sinclair is the first to react and nods the ball into the back of the net. Then Hughes goes one-on-one again, another excellent save, then it was Dobie's turn to be denied with his first touch, straight at the keeper.

Ladies and Gentlemen. This could be the beginning of the end. I sincerely hope it isn't, but it doesn't look good does it?

No Jason Roberts at Southampton, and James Beattie can't stop scoring!

Say no more!

Southampton away

Well I've heard some excuses in my time, but I think I can claim the prize this time! You see, we take it in turns driving to the away games, Stef, Andy, and myself. Not many away days left now, so we might have to draw straws to determine who drives to Sunderland – last away game, could be down and all that!!

Anyway, back to these excuses.... I think it was my turn to drive to Southampton and this is where I played my trump card. Being able to drive is one thing – it helps if you have a car though! No, I didn't smash it up or anything. Better than that! I sold it! The lengths some people will go to... (I was planning on selling it anyway; it just happened a bit quicker than I thought!)

Over to Andy. No, he'd been off ill for the last few days so he wasn't even coming with us. Stef, it looks like it's you son! Stef's car resembles a building site at the moment so we end up in Fay's car after all that. "Three is the magic number" so the De La Soul song goes and for the first time this year we were down to three in numbers. Dave's on his way back from Australia, Rich couldn't afford it, and Andy is ill. We carry on regardless!

The familiar trip down the M5, M42, and M40. Off at Junction 9 for Services and then through Newbury and the general direction of Southampton. Hour and half time expectations are more like two hours and thanks to www.awayguide.net, www.saintsfc.co.uk, and our loveable blue nose, Malc, we park up on the Travel Inn car park, 5 minutes walk from the ground. Walk towards the ground and enjoy the usual pre-match warm up of Lager, Lager, and a Guinness for Stef, regional cobs/baps/batches with a variety of fillings – far too much raw, eye watering, throat burning, freshly grown never mind cut, onions on mine! And of course, football on Sky. Post-match entertainment this week comes in the style of top-less barmaids from 5pm till 7pm. Now there's an idea!

Short walk to the impressive looking stadium and time to find our seats. Like I said, first impressions were good, then......
1. Our seats are at the end of the away section. No real reason to

moan.
2. We're about seven rows from front. Shitty view but not too bad.
3. Even though we have a spare seat, we're all squashed up because the steward can't be bothered to sort out people's tickets. A pain, but reasonable legroom.
4. The away fans are about 5 feet away with only a 3-foot high metal fence in the way. Oh dear. I hope it doesn't kick off!
5. It starts to rain. Brand new stadium and we're getting wet!

The game starts and then a few people decide to switch off! Firstly, the lines man on our side decides that the ball is still in play when I'm sure the bloke in the fifteenth row of the stand was about to pick it up and give it to Ife Udeze for a throw in. NO! Ok then, just play to the whistle. Then... "Ife, play to the whistle".... "Oi, Ife, he's run past you, get on with it"... Tefler passes to Ormerod, he chests it down to Beattie, 25-yard screamer, Hoult no chance!! Seven minutes gone, one nil down! I think we ARE going down! Ten minutes later, on comes Clement. Udeze must have pissed Megson off with his antics regarding the linesman, his lack of defending when we didn't have the ball and lack of attacking wing play when we did have the ball.

To be honest, I can't really remember much else from the first half. Albion were poor and apart from a free kick from Koumas, and half chances for Hughes and Gregan, there wasn't much to shout about at all. Hoult was the first half hero as he produced saves to keep out a 30 yarder and a close range volley.

The second half continued just as the first had finished. Hoult saving from Fernandez, pushing his shot onto the bar. In reply McInnes cleared the bar from 25 yards. What a surprise! Albion registered their first corner just after an hour so you can see what I mean when I say we lacked attacking pressure.

As is the case just lately, for the last 20 minutes Albion decide to start attacking the opposition's box. Why they don't try this tactic a bit earlier I'll never know! After Siggy had made a last ditch effort to keep out another Beattie shot, the ball went down the other end and Hughes was brought down in the area. He, along with

3,000 of us in the stands, was crying out for a penalty – let's just face it; we're not going to get a penalty this season!

Dichio then had the best chance to level the scores. An Albion corner saw a flick from Siggy; scuffed shot from Hughes and a half-shot from Dichio go agonisingly wide of the target. Another Dichio chance in the final minute, but it was blocked by a defender as it was heading for the corner of the net. We make our way back to the car but decide against the topless bar maids, they weren't letting any away fans back in the pub. All aboard for the journey back home, Burger Kings all round!

Strachan called us the gutsiest team in the league. Fair play to him I thought but guts only get you so far. Guts and ability take you places but when you lack genuine ability at the top level, guts buy you no more than admirers. So Strachan admired the Albion's heart did he? Will he still think the same after we are relegated? Will he care? Of course not, but such is life.

Chelsea home

21 points in total and 6 behind the team in the final safe place in the league. I think it's fair to say I'll be watching Nationwide football next year. I, for one, am angry with the odd decision by the odd referee and have little faith in the spendthrift board but the bottom line is my beloved Albion are not good enough and haven't been all season. I witnessed an acceptance today from the fans. I feel as though it was this sunny Sunday afternoon when we finally accepted that this season of fairytales and adventure was over, even if not mathematically. We have played with heart and honesty, had scant luck along the way and played very poorly in places but I would not have missed it for the world. I know this seems a little final and maybe premature but it feels right to say it now.

The back 5 was altered before kick off as Gilchrist was ruled out. It was further changed when Big Dave went down and didn't get up. It took 6 blokes to struggle with his stretcher along the Halfords Lane touchline!! I have now found out that he might be out as long as 9 months - can't believe it really, can you? As the game progressed I genuinely thought that Chelsea were here for the taking. Sunday afternoon stroll in the park is what they thought they would get, unfortunately for us, that is how it transpired. If we had scored first (I've mentioned that before somewhere, surely), Chelsea's desire would have undoubtedly been questioned. We didn't. 5 minutes before half time they had a corner, which was harmlessly floated over for the completely unmarked and equally unimpressive Stanic to head home. There was a time when I would have gone barmy at this point but it seemed to epitomise our season in an instant, a scenario I had become accustomed to, all too well. Poor, basic defending from a set piece. The whole crowd and playing staff also knew that 1 - 0 down meant game over. We played the second half like we have played the whole season. We huffed and puffed but the only breath in the stadium came in the form of an air of inevitability. I stared at the pitch, listened to moans at the "idle" Roberts and groans at Megson's tactics but couldn't help thinking that Chelsea's Jimmy

Floyd Hasselbank cost more than the entire Albion 11 (no I am not joking). Zola strutted his stuff and scored the second and final goal after a good move, albeit an obvious one to me. I'm not going to spend time eulogising over Zola like the pundits and press alike because I genuinely called the pass and move which lead to their goal but the Albion defence preferred to stand and watch.

The crowd responded to the defeat with an acceptance and air of resignation. We will be relegated at the end of the season just as, either Man Utd or Arsenal will be champions. It will be a time remembered by Albion fans and no one else because to be honest, who cares about West Brom? We slumped off knowing that we still had to make pretty meaningless trips to Sunderland and Middlesborough (do you realise how far these places are?). The Smethwick End sang Megson's name in a great showing of support and respect, they also made it clear to the players that the majority of us will be "Albion till we die" and have nothing but love for them. Funny thing football, sometimes I can simply take a step back and maturely and rationally accept my club's position. The other occasions have been touched upon throughout this journey.

I went home and looked at the fixtures. I could see the end in sight. I was quite sad and yet proud of my team and myself. We play the Blues on Saturday at 12pm in an effort to avoid trouble amongst the fans but I really can't see it.

Blues away

I once said if I didn't support the Albion I would follow the Blues. Funny really because some aspects of Birmingham City I really dislike whilst others I admire and am even drawn towards. At school there were only a handful of Blues fans if that, so no rivalry really set in there. To be honest, in the early 80s they were definitely the poor relations of Midland's football. We always seemed to beat the poor old Blues so I felt no animosity toward them, unlike their neighbours across the Expressway. When things were bad, me and my mates actually used to say "Well it could be worse, we could support the Blues!" This feeling continued for the most part of the late 80s and early 90s as we still had a great record against them. Then one sunny afternoon 6 of us got into our mates Metro (God knows how) and went to St Andrews for the first time. I was 18 and the others were either 16 or 17. We had no idea about parking and so just headed for the ground and looked about. We ended up finding a nice little spot on a side street and walked merrily to the ground. The game was in the old 3rd Division and both teams were towards the top. St Andrews was still pre-Taylor Report with a Kop on the side and behind both goals. The place was packed to the rafters for the first time in ages and a great atmosphere ensued. The Albion were magnificent and Bob Taylor in his prime. We won 3 - 0 and went top, seriously denting the Blues' hopes of promotion themselves. After the game we walked out the ground and began to retrace our steps to the car. Unfortunately for us, the Police refused entry to a road we had come down on the way to the ground so we had to be redirected round and about. After the enforced detour we turned the corner to be met by thousands of pretty pissed off Blue noses. It was like a scene from a film. They marched towards us and we stayed silent, trying in vein to be indiscriminate in our appearance. I just remember passing what seemed like the roughest section of society ever imaginable. Fan after fan was hard-faced and grimacing. They spat at us, yelled abuse, threatened to kill us. One bloke of about 50 elbowed my 16-year-old mate in his ribs and told him to "F off, Yam Yam scum". In turn, Blue noses asked where our colours were,

Baggie Bird at St. Andrews

knowing we were away fans by the direction we were walking. Another mate was shoved up a fence with an arm in his throat while I was "cuffed" round the back of my neck. This seemed to be person after person. Even women and smaller children hurled abuse and threatened us with violence. By the time we reached the car, it is fair to say I was a nervous wreck and my mates close to tears. The feeling I had for Birmingham City somewhat changed after that experience, shall we say.

I think the positive feeling I have for them is to do with a number of factors. Firstly, they hate Villa. A point not lost on me. Secondly it is true to say that we have shared a fair bit of hardship together. Losing to non-league opposition, 3rd Division football, financial difficulties and let down after let down. The 80s and 90s held pretty similar experiences for both Albion and Blues.

The game itself was so poor it was untrue. The Albion seemed either unable to get forward or were not prepared to. People around me began to question Megson's tactics, as we played so deep it was inevitable that we were not going to score. Blues were equally unimpressive. It was perfect conditions - sunny and bright with all to play for but both sides gave the impression they were resigned to their fate. Blues staying in the Premier for another season and the Albion dead and buried waiting for the end of the season. Durkin reffed reasonably well but he too missed some glaringly obvious decisions (did Devlin honestly get away with that push on Ballis??!!). Malc and me had exchanged pleasantries before the game via text and phone but there just wasn't the rivalry there. Singing was sporadic - lets face it the Blues had finished their season now. Safe, barring a miracle of Biblical proportions and they had done the league double over the Vile (5 - 0 on aggregate). The visit of the Albion was an out of date after dinner mint at the end of a wonderful 4-course meal. Just while I'm thinking about it, I thought it was a nice touch for the teams to come out behind a Union Jack in support of our troops in Iraq. I'm pretty sure it was the first show of positive public feeling about the conflict since the whole thing began. We are regularly bombarded with negative press because it sells, but the silent majority, who don't feel as though there is any need to go out and march etc. to air their views, were certainly heard Saturday morning.

The 4th official held up the board and indicated 4 minutes extra to play at the end of the 90. I was somewhat puzzled at this but thought nothing of it. That was until exactly (well, it must have been, according to Durkin's watch) 93 mins and 55 seconds - I'm not joking! Blues pressure saw a looping cross come over for sub Horsefield to nod into the bottom corner with a tame header. Durkin blew for full time after the second touch of the ball from the restart. I refused to stay to see the Blues go barmy, I just couldn't stomach it. Needless to say the chants of "going down" were ringing out immediately. Furthermore, it is also needless to report that there was no trouble (Blues won didn't they?). We got back to the car and like the impression the Albion players gave - forgot about it as soon as possible and dreamt of Grimsby, etc. The Dream itself is all but over. At the time of writing it seems a bit disappointing to be honest. The season started as an adventure, it's now beginning to seem a chore.

I thought the Red Indians of Nevada had bought this?

Smithy decides to have yet another burger

Middlesborough away

Well this is a new venture for all of us, I think, the Riverside Stadium, or Cellnet Stadium, or whatever they call it these days! But on first impressions, the bridge from the last series of Auf Wiedersehen got more attention. No honestly, if you'd have taken the huge badges down from the stadium walls we could have been going to Sunderland, Man Utd, Southampton, anywhere really. But don't get me wrong; these grounds are fantastic from the inside. Brilliant views from every seat; no uprights to hold up the roof and obstruct your view; a fair amount of legroom (still need a bit more though!) and plenty of room for a pint!

However, still on the inside, the toilets are stupidly small. Now, over the years I have had the misfortune to notice, on several occasions, home and away, gentlemen feeling the need to urinate in the sinks to save waiting in the queue. This I agree is disgusting, but at Middlesborough, to my horror and, strangely enough, amusement, I notice a teenage Baggie feeling the urge to piss, not in the urinal, not even in the sink, but on the floor next to the sink! No comment!!

Now the outside! All of the grounds these days consist of a big grey and white structure with white scaffolding round the roof; very bland and no character. Everton has the same set up just blue roof supports. Even the Wolves is just the same structure but obviously lots of orange paint everywhere.

Wait a minute, how did the Dingles get a mention? I thought this book was about the Premier League!

All through the season we've had plenty to moan about, but here's another. Fixtures. Obviously, it would be a little different if we were a bit higher up in the table, but who's idea was it to play away at Middlesborough on the 5th, then Everton at home on the 12th, then back up to Sunderland on the 19th. They're only 30 miles apart! I think the idea of flying to Newcastle was an excellent one, is there an airport at Sunderland?

So we arrive in Middlesborough with directions from the Internet. Decide to find the ground, even though Bluenose Malc has already told Stef "If you see the ground – you've gone too far!" Ok then. Let's try and find a pub then, no Andy wants to know where the ground is. We keep looking and finally ask a local. It's further than we thought and "there's no match day parking near the ground". Turn round back to the multi-storey car park. Can't park on first 75 floors due to short stay only. We decide in the end we could get away with short stay till about 6pm. Then this kind Northerner lets us have his ticket. Cheers mate – long stay floors only! Up another 15 or so floors! Half way down, have you got the tickets? – no they're in the car. This could be a long day!!

After watching the Man Utd v Liverpool game in the pub, but missing the penalty, we make our way to the ground. Which way? I don't honestly know! We just followed some blokes wearing Middlesborough scarves. Through some shops, past some students trying to get an anti-war demo going, er no! Through "Merry Hill", past one car park, under a subway, past another car park, stop for a burger – that's better, isn't it Paul? – under another subway, over an island. There's the Bridge, and there's the ground! About time too!

As for the game, we were shit! No real desire, no attacking formation, nobody really marking Juninio! Do I need to say more? Oh and then, surprise surprise, they score. Now remember, Albion didn't look like they were going to score one let alone two! Which reminds me; predictions were 1-0, 2-1, 3-0, and 4-0 all in favour of Boro surprisingly. Well that's it then, could this be the week of our doom? Malcolm Christie, of all people, gets the first. After Albion had nearly signed him earlier in the season!

Hoult was the only player to come out with any credit in the first half after pulling off a few saves. After the break this continued in much the same way! A brilliant tip over and then a double save which would have had Mr Eriksson asking some questions if only we were higher up in the table; but you don't pick an England keeper from a team who are going down, do you?

Jonathon Greening was than given time and space to play one-twos with virtually everyone in the stadium, including the Albion back three, before slotting the ball past the oncoming Hoult. Time to go guys!

As we leave the ground we get the usual remarks of "all the best for next year, it's a shame your going down – you'll be straight back up next year!" Then Stef decided to go for the Best Look-a-Like of the Day Award with Graeme Souness. Unfortunately, he won hands down, mainly because it was him! After a quick turn of the head, he was in his chauffeur driven car and out of here!

Now, if you remember it was a long walk to the ground, so we decided on another first for the season – a taxi to the car park. Well, we did get to hear the rest of the match on the radio – including the third goal! As we approach the car parks, Andy, to our amusement, starts to give the taxi driver directions. Bearing in mind we live near Birmingham, we're in a taxi in Middlesborough and quite obviously, the taxi driver is from Middlesborough. Just sit back and relax Smithy, let him do his job! It's your turn to drive in a minute – all the way home!

Well, due to results elsewhere, we're still not mathematically down. But I've started to give out the invitations to the Relegation Party next week at the Hawthorns at 4.45pm. Special guest is Wayne Rooney and his pals from the blue half of Merseyside..................

Everton home

So this is it, the fat lady is on the stage and having a final gargle before she starts singing! Keep your arms and legs inside the vehicle at all times and hold on tight! We might go down today – depends on how we handle Mr Rooney!

After the first breakfast down the golf club for absolutely ages, a quick visit to the Wernley, and then off to the ground. Sweets and choc from the corner shop accompanying the usual comment "You win today?" - no mate we're on our way to the game……..Oh never mind stick to United or Liverpool.

The game started in its usual up-beat manner. Albion on the attack from the first whistle, why they haven't done this all season I'll never know, and Dichio crashes a header against the bar after 5 minutes. Then Siggy pokes the rebound wide! Typical, a defender in an attacking position!!

Then enter Wayne Rooney, first nut-megs Wallwork but then shoots over from just inside area. "You'll never play for England!" roars the Albion faithful. More good attacking play by the Albion allow Dichio another header towards goal and then McInnes sets up Koumas on the edge of the area. Wright holding Koumas' well-struck volley with ease.

Now, remember I told you to hold on to your seats, well Dichio and Stubbs tussle for the ball in the area and Stubbs brushes the ball away with his hand… surely… come on ref.… YES, there it is, the lesser-spotted penalty in favour of the Baggies. Now, what next? Hughes wants to take it. Balis wants it. Hughes is playing very well but if you recall it is nearly a year ago to the day that Igor scored that all-important penalty at Bradford last season. Over to you, Balis!

GOOOOOOOOOAL!!!!!!! Get in there!

But alas, typical Albion. Not even 5 minutes later, Doddy Weir, near post corner, beats Hoult, one each!

Hughes was playing like a man possessed. He skipped past Unsworth but Richard Wright covered his left foot strike. Hughes then cut inside Unsworth again and squared the ball across the face of the goal where Johnson managed to attempt a Riverdance manoeuvre but failed to put the ball in the back of the empty goal. Hoult was then at full stretch to keep out a Rooney lob and to stir things up a little, David Moyes was ordered out of his dugout for 'effin this and that at the linesman prior to half time.

Just after the restart it was like deja vu. Hughes crosses from the right across the face of goal but this time Wallwork is unable to connect. Does this sum up the season or what?

Then the killer blow we have come to expect these days. Hoult fumbled a corner and the ball fell to the feet of Rooney who passed to Campbell for an easy shot at goal. Two goals – two real shots on target!

But as the game progressed, Albion as usual, had the better chances to turn the game around. Clement got the ball mixed up in his feet after a fine run, Balis delayed when Dichio was expecting a cross when he was unmarked in the box. Then a great reaction effort from Hughes held again by Wright and then Dichio volleyed narrowly wide after a cross from Balis.

Another defeat, another game we could have and possibly should have won. It's hard but it's goals that count not chances!
I think that could be it – does anyone know any scores from elsewhere?

Sunderland away

So that is that. The dream is now officially over, the Albion were relegated at the final whistle today. Was it relief or indifference? I'm not sure because the feeling was very strange as the Bolton result filtered through. Truth is I knew we were down some time ago so it didn't come as a surprise, there were no last day tears or heartache here. To add to the bizarre feeling we only went and won 2 - 1!! The whole occasion had a surreal feel to it. Sunderland were already relegated and couldn't care one bit, we were down but for mathematics and there were no permutations to eagerly consider before or during the game. 200 miles of travelling each way with a sell out Albion section (unbelievable) of fans who all seemed to reflect my feeling of acceptance made for a truly strange day. The last relegation experience was awful. Bristol Rovers, toga party, Bobby Gould, Leicester City, last day, etc. Awful, a truly awful experience (how it should be I suppose). Not today though, we all knew what was waiting round the corner and that our time with the Big Boys was coming to an end. My biggest disappointment perhaps, is the fact that we couldn't take it to the wire. The drama, the intrigue, nerves, clock watching, radio hugging last day scenario. I also worry about our chances next year to be honest. I'm not one of these who think we will wipe the floor in the lower league (Wigan, Watford??) so perhaps it's a time to reflect on one year in my life when I could say the Baggies were one of the top teams in the country but that's the end of it.

The game itself was quite good really. We played well and deserved to go in front even though Hoult pulled off a great save early on. McInnes made sure after a defensive mix up from close range. Soon after it was 2 as McInnes again (can't believe that) followed up a deflected free kick to scramble home. We boinged and sang but my heart didn't seem in it. Sunderland pulled one back but we held firm to record our third away win of the season - sixth win in total. Bolton beat West Ham 1 - 0 so couldn't be caught by us even if we won our last 4 and they lost theirs. Fitting I suppose that our Premier life died the day after Good Friday. My concern, however, is who's going to help us rise again? The past week was again (shock) filled with Boardroom rumblings with Mr Thompson saying one thing and Mr Peace rebuking another. Upshot of it all is, Peace has bought Thompson's shares and is the major shareholder of the football club. I personally don't give a monkey's who the chairman is as long as we spend a reasonable amount of cash in the summer rebuilding the team and investing in youth (Yeah right, like that's gonna happen).

The car on the way back needed constant air freshening as the boys continued to emit bodily gases as a warning to what lay in wait for the toilets on the services and at home. The four of us spent the whole day eating crap, drinking and doing daft bets. Closest to the attendance figure, score, goalscorers and the usual "Corners", basically we tried very hard to liven up a desperate day. I don't know, perhaps in the future I will look back and change my mind about this venture. I mean the Albion won, the ground is great, we had a laugh, etc. but it just wasn't right. I don't think it has been for some time now. When you see 30 odd games and only a handful of victories it takes its toll. Add to that the lack of media interest in the club and the inactivity in the transfer market along with too much negative football and no inclination to change it from the manager and well, you know the rest. The real downer this season has been the realisation that we would be relegated as early as November time. When you know your club is not going to buy in January and the players you have at the moment are not good enough going to matches knowing you're going to lose is not much fun for months on end. In a funny way we've had nothing to play for, for ages now it seems. Good old West Brom, they've tried hard haven't they? Honest pros with big hearts, shame, etc. more pity, etc. Make no mistake, the Premier League is the place to be. But by the same score, it is not the place to be whipping boys every week. Losing at any level is not nice. Oh well roll on Rotherham, Wigan and Walsall goodbye United, Arsenal and Liverpool. Hello midweek footy, half-empty stadiums and zero media coverage, so long 50,000 sell outs, Sky TV and ITV. Please to meet you A N Other, J Bloggs and N O Body, all the best Giggs, Henry and Owen. I feel a bit down as you've probably guessed but in time I will soon realise that it doesn't matter because we were there. My Baggies played one year in the top flight of English football, the best league in the world and I was there to see them.

Spurs home

So here we go for the first home game after relegation. Sunderland was such a confidence booster, and now we know that we are playing for pride not survival, I think today's game could be quite a good one - just that slight problem of Robbie Keane. A few beers before the game and then a couple of bets at the ground. Now we all know that Keane will score and with all the stick we'll give him about Wolves, he'll want to score even more. Therefore, the idea of a win to nil is soon squashed! This betting lark doesn't seem so bad when we don't need to win – but it would be nice if we did!

Koumas was the first to test the American keeper but his 35-yard effort was easily held. Roberts jinxed his way past Dean Richards a few minutes later but miss-hit his cross to Dichio. Hoult saved the defender's blushes as he tipped an overhead attempt by Keane past the upright.

Gardener was then booked for pulling back Roberts outside the box but after the free kick had been half cleared, a Koumas cross found it's way onto the head of Mr. Dichio. Brilliant. 1 - 0. Could get used to this!

Johnson shot straight at Keller from the edge of the box after half an hour. And Johnson then set up McInnes with a well-timed header, to put a Roberts' cross into his path. Keller scrambled across his goal but fingertipped the ball away from McInnes' 18-yard effort. Johnson had to turn his attention to defending shortly after that, and his timely intervention prevented Bunjevcevic from levelling the scores.

Unfortunately, they did level the scores with virtually the last kick of the first half. Keane and Sheringham linked well together before the former Man Utd star chipped a ball over the static Albion defence. Need I say any more? Keane. 1-1.

Dingle father-less person!

Roberts came close at the start of the second half after a surging run and fine exchange on the edge of the box with Balis. His weak shot rather let him down.

Poyet squandered a chance as the defence parted like the Red Sea, after good work by Etherington on the right. Then it was Koumas' chance to turn on the style. His mazy run came to a halt 25 yards out when he was brought down. Roberts flicked his quick free kick on but Keller managed to push the shot over the bar.

Then I'm not sure if it was tactical or whether Udaze had nearly hit the corner flag with a shot, but on came Clement seconds before we were awarded another free kick 35 yards or so out. Due to Richards' protesting at the decision, he was booked and the ball was moved forwards 10 yards. Step up Neil Clement. Second touch and a scorcher of a free kick, straight past Keller. Fantastic!

But just like Everton, within a few minutes, we've let a goal go in. Keane's miscued free kick is headed back across goal by that foreign bloke I mentioned earlier, that Bunjev bloke, the ball rebounds off the bar and falls into the path of Sheringham. He's not going to miss from a couple of yards, is he?

After Roberts had his shot charged down and Stephen Carr made sure Hoult was still awake, we almost had a re-run of Keane's goal at White Hart Lane. A clever ball over the heads of Gregan and Sigurdson enabled Keane to race between then and slot the ball past Hoult from 10 yards out.

Yes again it could be said, a game we could have won, but definitely a game we shouldn't have lost! Not many games left now and there's a certain points total we need to pass. Watford have the record for the lowest points in the Premier League – 24.

Now we don't want to set a new record now do we??

Liverpool home

For the first time this season in the league I questioned the Albion players and their commitment. I heard all the excuses about us already being relegated and nothing to play for but the performance they gave in this game was nothing short of disgusting in my opinion. Admittedly, we were without all three recognised centre halves so had two midfielders and a left back playing there but that's no excuse for the embarrassment I witnessed. I know motivation for a meaningless (to some) game might be difficult but this was Liverpool FC, the most successful club of all time - what an opportunity? We gave up from the first whistle, waiting for something to happen, looking at eachother and dreaming of a beach somewhere, I guess. The ground was packed again to the rafters but I for one, felt so let down it was untrue. I don't want to hear that Liverpool are a class act and Michael Owen is this and Gerrard is that. Better than us they are, but letting them play is something totally different. Don't remember Blues being a soft touch against them the other week, do you? I was so angry it was unbelievable. Gerrard's body language said it all. He strutted in front of the Smethwick with an air of control and arrogance that just oozed a feeling of "So what?" or "Where the hell am I?" He even had time to snigger because basically he was playing a Sunday League team without the "get stuck-in" mentally.

The atmosphere was either fantastic or ridiculous, depending on your point of view. I for one, could not believe the majority of fans who sounded their love for the team at the end of the game. Talk about blind passion. I never complain about player's wages, etc. but here were 11 blokes earning an absolute fortune simply not doing their job and seemed to not care in the slightest either. Not one rash tackle out of petulance either! How the hell could I clap after seeing that gutless showing? There were thousands of fans clapping and singing like we had won the league - most loyal in the division or stupidest? You decide. I hadn't felt like this for years. Defeat is not nice but to go out like a limping dog without a whimper is not something I was about to applaud. Some blokes think they are more of a fan if they never criticise or question and stay "loyal to the lads". Crap!

They had given up, I hadn't. I still went, had paid my money, given my support, etc. but for nothing it seemed.

I had been in the pub prior to the game and was talking to Scouse (Liverpool fan, funnily enough). He was a little concerned that his beloved were going to lose to the second worst team in the country and never live it down - they had already lost to the Blues don't forget! I reassured him that there was more chance of the missus going off chocolate. Then I went on to discuss our season very briefly. My main points were our lack of goals, hard work ethic, Megson's perceived preference to bollock rather than talk tactics, terrible refereeing decisions against us and the fact that we still hadn't really copped for a pasting. He smiled and said in jest, "Why not today then?" How ironic that last statement proved to be, aye? We were one-nil down at half time after Owen latched on to a through ball and left our "defence" for dead. Other than that we had a 15-minute spell where we huffed and puffed in our usual manner without blowing the Scouse swine's house down. The second half was nothing short of embarrassing comedy. Barros, who I don't rate as highly as some incidentally, took us to the cleaners on more than one occasion for a quick wash. Owen, who will be a Liverpool legend and could be one at international level too, had more room than when he played for North Wales schoolboys. Gerrard had enough time in midfield to hand roll a Cuban cigar before he picked a team mate out. Hypia, who I still haven't forgiven for his GBH on Roberts at Anfield (nice one Ellery), could have spent the majority of the afternoon in a deck chair only to head clear the odd cross. Dudek, are you sure that's not Ian Rush? may as well have had a £10 lap dance in the second half in front of the Brummie Road for all the pressure he was under. The list goes on. Basically, the whole Liverpool 11 could have played in flippers, on the wrong feet, with their legs tied and carrying a bag of cement each and still beat the Albion.

Just for the record we lost 6 - 0. Our biggest home defeat for God knows how long. Whether we were relegated or not that result stands, it's in the record book, it counts. What players seem to forget is, we fans have to go to work after that and face ridicule. Losing is one thing but that was a joke you couldn't defend. Thanks lads.

Blackburn away

Now I'm not sure who put forward the idea for the Last Away Game Fancy Dress, but I don't think they had to put too much thought into it... Men In Black... Referees!!

Now, I knew that the Smith twin's wouldn't really enter into this side of the entertainment, but Stef and I decided to do our bit by wearing our Afro wigs. Not quite warm enough for shorts at the moment but some brave souls were wearing them. Quiz Master Roy, from the Wernley had offered me his referee's top but couldn't find it in time!

Fortunately, Andy had talked Dave Price into going to this game and therefore would drive. Great, the four of us could all have a drink together for a change.

Unfortunately, the day before the game, Dave had phoned Andy to say that he wouldn't be going, bad back or something. This would normally be a reasonable excuse, but Dave has had a bad back for the last 5 years so it must have been pretty bad!

So here we go, last Premiership trip up the M6. Shame really, I've got quite used to this, if we do decide to get away tickets next season I don't think we'll be going to them all. It's just nice to not have to queue for tickets all the time. We'll definitely go to some but Norwich on a Tuesday night doesn't really excite me that much! We arrive in plenty of time to watch the Man Utd game in the referee's local. Well, there were so many people dressed up outside that it may well have been!

There were referees with pink hair; referees with pony tails; referees with glasses and bald heads; even a Hitler referee! Red and yellow cards of all shapes and sizes, with plenty being passed around for those who had come without. Even the local constabulary was enjoying the banter, as long as we didn't go on the road. They were even videoing the fans, but I don't think it was because they were amused by our outfits, probably more to do with the amount of alcohol that was being consumed.

We battle our way to the bar, battle our way to the toilets, battle our way out of the pub, battle our way to the ground and finally battle our way to our seats. Well this year has been one giant battle and in an effort of unity and solidarity it can now be said that the fans had to battle against the referees as well as the players!!!!!!! The game itself wasn't much to write home about ……so what am I doing now then…?

It turned out to be another battle in itself, a battle between Koumas and Damien Duff. Even though they were not marking each other, their skilful runs cancelled each other out with both players ending up with a goal each (and the praises of the pundits on the Premiership!)

Most of the Albion fans spent most of the game chanting obscene songs about the Premier League and its army of officials, a little over the top at times but highly amusing and entertaining! However, apart from the Albion equaliser, of course, the loudest cheer of the day was for the "mascots" at the front of the stand. They weren't these ridiculous team mascots, which have to parade around before and after the matches, no, some people had actually taken the trouble to hire costumes for the day!

We had a penguin, an anteater, a dodgy version of Eeyore and the star of the show, a giraffe! It wasn't the warmest of days and

Look carefully and you will see Gav!

Clive Whitehead and Remi Moses at Blackburn

it's a good job, they must have been roasting in those costumes. Mind you they did a valiant attempt of organising a conga before the stewards asked them to return to their seats. Seats! Seats! No, let's just remember where we are! We're at an away game, which means we spend all game standing up and sit down at half time, if we can be bothered, and more-to-the-point it's the last away game so I can't really see what the problem is. If it's because people might not be able to see, then I suggest they take off their Jobs-worth caps for a moment and take a look around!

There are enough red and yellow cards to fill the surface of the pitch and so many inflatables you could mistake the place for a Spanish holiday resort! Now I don't think the Albion fans are going to complain too much really!

Souness might have other feelings though, his side needs to win to be certain of playing in Europe next year.

Albion, on the other hand, just need to turn up to be certain of playing in the Nationwide next year!!

A good all round performance by the Albion gave us a deserved point to take back with our final memories of our first and hopefully not our last season in the big league.

Newcastle United home

The performance at Blackburn helped exorcise some of the demons of the Liverpool game a couple of weeks ago but relatively few Albion fans witnessed it. It is for this reason that I really wanted the Albion to perform today. Last game, Bob Taylor and all that. We have been praised all season for our support of, basically, a lost cause. The English public loves the underdog, the loser, the one with no chance. The media hadn't exactly chosen us in this respect but many pointed to our support for a special mention. I for one, am not totally convinced by this. Praise from Des Lynam and Ally McCoist is one thing but listening to it from local Villa and in particular "Big Club Blues" fans on radio phone-ins is too condescending for me. Bottom line, however, is overall, our fans have been magnificent this season in the fruitless quest of the survival-Holy Grail.

Newcastle came to town with a Champions League place in the bag with nothing to play for except their fans. We had been down for some time now so the game was rather a side show to a true modern day legend. To see Bob Taylor's name in the starting line up threw me totally. I had spent all week castigating Megson for his treatment of Super Bob and kept asking people why he wouldn't give him a shirt for the last game. So what does Megson do? Pick him from the start - fair play, I apologise.

Every club has a hero. Somebody who has earned the right to gain your respect. They usually have to meet certain criteria. Honesty, hard working, bravery, dignity and above all loyalty. If a player meets these and is a goal scorer too, it often elevates them to legend status. Allowing for a brief spell at Bolton, Bob Taylor has been at the Albion for 10 years. In this time he has never let the club down once. I remember his debut when he scored against Brentford at the Hawthorns and the hat full he got that season in the old third division. It wasn't just the number of goals he got that made him special though. He scored important goals. Who remembers his equaliser at Molineux when they had a star studded side? His diving header against the Wolves in front of the Smethwick? His goals against

Bolton when we nearly went down a couple of years ago? Forest away last year? The winner against Palace that sent us up? Away from his goals came his relentless running for the cause. He got stuck in and never bottled a fight. We loved Bob Taylor for many reasons but perhaps the biggest of all was the fact that he loved us. He always left the field last and clapped every section of the ground, away fans too more often than not. He was good for a laugh, warm and accessible when interviewed and regularly spoke of his appreciation for us, the fans. He sat amongst us last week in the away section at Blackburn wearing a Ref's uniform to blend in with the thousands of others for a laugh - need I say more? The word legend is bounded about too often to be honest. Best is a legend, Matthews is a legend, Charlton and Moore are legends but I promise you, as they are adored around the world, Bob Taylor is adored in exactly the same way around by us. Bob Taylor is a legend. It is for this reason, that when his name was read out before the game and the ground erupted to sing his name, I could not take part for the lump in my throat.

The game itself was poor in the first half only to come alive after the break. By this time the hero of the day had ironically gone off injured and his replacement, Dobie had scored to cancel out Jenas's opener and struck again to put us 2 - 1 up! Although they were without Shearer and Bellamy, Newcastle still had enough quality to hurt us. Hurt us they did before the end when Viana hit a free kick that beat Hoult to make it 2 - 2. Oh well, not to worry. We played with our heart and gained some respect back. I sat and pondered at the final whistle like I did 12 months ago on that amazing day last April. Strangely enough, there was a pitch invasion and celebrations a little similar to give me more to contemplate. The end of the Premiership line. No more stops, everyone off please. This train terminates here and will start again in August, but you won't be on it this time. The curtain fell and our year in the top flight of the best league in the world was over. We gave it our all but this was never going to be enough. I was sad that it was finished, as opposed to our relegation. In hindsight, our adventures together have been brilliant, especially away from home but now they have come to an end and it is slowly beginning to hurt. We took our last photos and slowly trudged out of our home for the last time this season. Next year we are being moved back to the other side of the Smethwick so our seats went too. What an unbelievable year in the life of a West Bromwich Albion fan. Just hope it isn't another 16 till we do it all again.

Epilogue

What a year. The highs and the lows, the laughter and anger, we've had it all. It's been simply incredible, a journey that has taken us from Southampton to Newcastle and back. 38 games later and the Premiership train has made its last stop. There have been times when I questioned my blind passion, when I longed for my bed and when I felt despair at what I was witnessing but next game I was back. An irrepressible force that controls you in a way never witnessed before. Match day is like nothing else. Away days even more so. The laughs we've had are untrue - parking at Newcastle and Fulham, the taxi in Boro, the bloke on the labour club door in Newcastle, the crisps at Man City, seeing Shaft at Chelsea, wigs at Blackburn, the hotel attendant at Southampton - the list goes on. It soon became apparent that the football was going to play second fiddle to the day itself away from home. Albion let me down and then again, they didn't if you know what I mean. Nobody really expected anything more than relegation but then perhaps the club could have been a little more adventurous in the transfer market, I don't know.

Anyway - "best of" awards:

- Best goal (Albion) - Scott Dobie Bolton away
- Best goal (other) - Beattie Southampton away
- Best ground - St James Park
- Not best ground - Fulham (what ground?)
- Best fans away - Chelsea
- Best fans at the Albion - Man Utd
- Not best fans away - anyone from Blackburn, Liverpool, Fulham, Villa
- Not best fans at the Albion - Sunderland
- Best kit - Spurs at home
- Not best kit - Arsenal away (gold?)
- Best pub - the Archal at Anfield

- Not best pub - Bowling Alley at Bolton
- Best day out - Chelsea, Tube? What's one of them Smithy?
- Not best day out - Fulham, a sarnie cost me £4 on the services at 11pm
- Best player - Robbie Keane (every bloody time!)
- Not best player - Campo, surely you've seen his hairpiece?
- Best atmosphere at the Albion - Villa, us not them
- Not best atmosphere at the Albion - Charlton
- Best atmosphere away - Chelsea
- Not best atmosphere away - Liverpool or Fulham
- Best moment - Koumas goal at Villa, I passed out
- Not best moment - the 2nd minute of injury time at Villa, I passed out
- Best referee - don't worry I'm taking the piss
- Best view - Newcastle, I could see Denmark
- Not best view - Everton, my back still hurts
- Best laugh - crisps at Man City, ask the lads
- Not best laugh - Man City hooligan element, I've had loose bowel movement ever since

So there we have it a seasons review, a year in the life, whatever you want to call it it's over now. See you next year.

Seasons Facts:

Games Attended: . . . . .40 (inc 2 FA Cup)
Grounds Visited: . . . . . .21 (inc. Hawthorns and Watford FA Cup)

Total Miles: . . . . .4450. . . . . (inc home games) 4850
Average Miles per Gallon: 45
Litres per Gallon: 4.5
Average Miles per Litre: 10
Price per Litre: . . . . .79 pence
Approx Petrol Cost: . . . . .£351.00 . . . . . . (inc home games) £383.00

Average Burgers/Fried Breakfasts Per Game: 2
Approx Amount of Burgers Consumed: 80
Average Burger Price: £2.50
Approx Food Costs: £200.00

Average Pints Per Game: 3
Approx Amount of Pints Consumed: 120
Average Pint Price: £1.95
Approx Drink Costs: £234.00

Average Price of Program: £2.50
Approx Cost of Programs: £100.00

Home Season Ticket: £252.00
Away Season Ticket: £120.00
Away Match Tickets: £294.00

Total approximate cost of following the Albion this year: . . . .
. . . .£1583.00 each